AF469237

Wellington Commander

THE IRON DUKE'S GENERALSHIP

Edited by
PADDY GRIFFITH

ANTONY BIRD PUBLICATIONS LIMITED
in association with
THE WELLINGTON MUSEUM

Published by Antony Bird Publications Limited
of Strettington House, Strettington, Chichester, Sussex
in association with The Wellington Museum

Designed and produced by Patrick Yapp
Maps by Nick Nicklinson
Printed in Great Britain by Butler & Tanner Ltd, Frome and London

British Library Cataloguing in Publication Data

Wellington-Commander: the Iron Duke's generalship
1. Wellington, Arthur Wellesley, *Duke of*
2. Great Britain. *Army*—Biography
3. Generals—Great Britain—Biography
I. Griffith, Paddy
941.07′092′4 DA68.12.W4

ISBN 0-907319-08-4

REVERSE OF FRONTISPIECE: The Wellington shield, designed by
Thomas Stothard RA (1755–1834) and made by
Benjamin Smith in about 1834.
FRONTISPIECE: This famous portrait of Wellington was painted
in August 1812, after his victory at Salamanca by Goya (1746–1828),
reproduced by courtesy of the Trustees, The National Gallery, London.

Contents

List of Colour Plates

NOTE: *The page numbers given are those opposite the colour plates, or, in the case of a double-page spread, those either side of the plate.*

List of Maps

Apsley House in early Victorian times, overshadowed by the huge statue of the Duke cast from his captured guns. Such exception was taken to this ungainly sculpture that it was soon discreetly moved to Aldershot.

Foreword

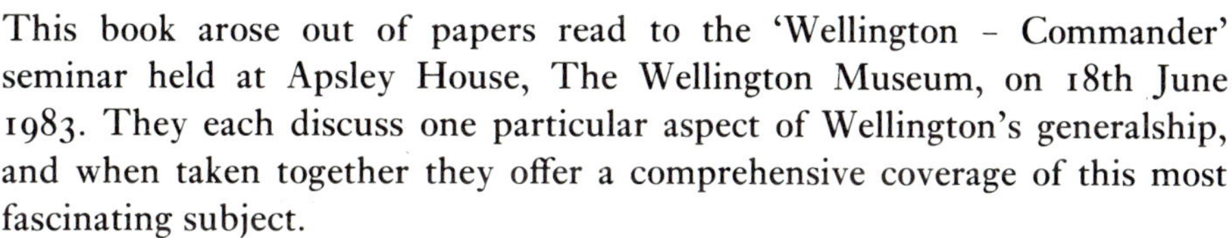

This book arose out of papers read to the 'Wellington – Commander' seminar held at Apsley House, The Wellington Museum, on 18th June 1983. They each discuss one particular aspect of Wellington's generalship, and when taken together they offer a comprehensive coverage of this most fascinating subject.

The first three chapters deal with Wellington's skills as a commander at the higher, or 'strategic', level of military action. In my general review of his campaigning life I try to show how his technique evolved from year to year, and especially how his changing attitudes to offensive and defensive forms of warfare were moulded by his different experiences. Michael Glover continues this theme by demolishing the myth that Wellington was a timid and defensive commander in the Peninsula. He reminds us of the manpower shortages and other pressures under which Wellington was forced to operate, and goes on to furnish some telling examples of Wellington as an attacker – a commander who could be called anything except 'timid'. John Terraine concludes this section with a study of Wellington's skilful handling of his allies in India, in the Peninsula and finally at Waterloo. He adds depth to his analysis by making a comparison with the abilities in alliance warfare of various Western commanders in the two World Wars. He shows that in these respects Wellington may sometimes have been equalled but was never surpassed.

The second part looks in some depth at Wellington's greatest triumph, the battle of Waterloo. David Howarth explains how the Mont St Jean position came to be chosen, how the British troops were concealed within it and how they were able to fight so effectively from it. This essay, in fact, makes a concise summary of the battle as a whole. John Keegan next lists, in meticulous detail, the Duke's personal movements on that fatal and enormously eventful day. He describes how Wellington adopted the 'heroic' style of battlefield command – placing himself always where the dangers were greatest – in sharp contrast to Napoleon's more 'managerial' (not to say entirely torpid) approach to the problem. Correlli Barnett then picks up this recurrent theme and mercilessly itemises the Emperor's mistakes.

He places Waterloo in the context of Bonaparte's other operations and concludes that it was by no means an untypical performance. With both Howarth and Keegan, therefore, Correlli Barnett casts his vote in favour of the view that Wellington was the better of the two opposing commanders at Waterloo.

There was little dissent from this opinion, in the Apsley House seminar, as far as Waterloo itself was concerned. A number of Bonapartist voices did nevertheless make themselves heard when it came to the wider question of whether Wellington or Napoleon had been the better commander overall. They reminded us that in a seminar of this nature, taking place under Wellington's own roof and surrounded by his magnificent trophies, there was inevitably a strong temptation to kick the unhappy Emperor when he was down. Wellington himself had always been very scathing about Napoleon's character and had graphically referred to him as 'Jonathan Wild the Great' (after Fielding's description of the king of thieves): yet we are not obliged either to accept Wellington's word on the matter or, indeed, to assume that a king of thieves will inevitably make a poor commander of armies. Least of all will this be the case when it transpires that he all but conquered the whole of continental Europe from one end to the other.

The debate about the respective merits of Wellington and Napoleon marked the strongest point of disagreement between members of the seminar. There were nevertheless several other disagreements over details, and not every lecturer concurred with every other lecturer all the time. The attentive reader will doubtless identify these points of difference readily enough – for example Michael Glover's interpretation of the battle of Busaco

Wellington addressing one of the annual Waterloo banquets in the Waterloo gallery, Apsley House. Many of the paintings were recaptured for the King of Spain at Vitoria, but then awarded to Wellington in recognition of his services.

is not the same as my own, and David Howarth differs from John Keegan on Wellington's itinerary before Waterloo. Such variations in emphasis, however, are inseparable from the process of historical writing. No effort is made here to resolve them, since it is felt that the presentation of several alternative interpretations adds a certain texture and depth to our understanding.

The final section of the book draws the focus down to the lower, or 'tactical' level of military action. In chapter 7 I examine the so-called 'thin red line' which has often been claimed as one secret of Wellington's success, and I attempt to show that its inner workings have been misrepresented in the past. Finally Graeme Rimer describes the various weapons which the British used in Napoleonic times, their effectiveness, methods of use and rates of fire.

By the end of the seminar we found that Wellington's glory had by no means diminished, and in certain areas it had rather tended to increase. Yet at the same time we had gained a broader understanding of his genius than many of us had previously enjoyed, which helped us to see him as a more comprehensible personality than in the past. New life was breathed into our impressions of a man who has too often been portrayed in a very stiff and stylised manner.

This volume allows the reader to share some of the new insights which we gained in the course of the seminar.

P.G.
Sandhurst, October 1983

PART ONE

Wellington and Strategy

CHAPTER 1

Wellington – Commander

PADDY GRIFFTH

No biographer can ever fully tear himself away from admiration of his subject, least of all when that subject happens to be a superlatively successful military commander. Such a figure fits too neatly into the archetypal definition of a 'hero' to leave us totally unmoved, and particularly if he fails to display those vices of recklessness, blood lust or greed which have tarnished the names of so many great captains throughout history.

The career of the Duke of Wellington apparently offers us a perfect example of the unblemished military life. He never lost a battle – which is rather more than we can say of Frederick, Napoleon or Lee – and he is not commonly remembered for waging war upon civilians – which should set him somewhat higher than Sherman, Ludendorff or their all too numerous disciples in more recent times. Wellington's political understanding was excellent, his logistics were superb and his intelligence work was magnificent. As a disciplinarian he was legendary, while as a tactician he was unsurpassed. In practically every branch of the military art, it would appear, his ability and energy were outstanding. It therefore seemed to come as a perfectly apt and fitting capstone to his military career that at Waterloo he should meet and defeat no less a military genius than Napoleon himself, with the result that Europe – enslaved no more – could throw off the oppression of war and sport joyously for a hundred years in the beneficent radiance of freedom, tranquillity and progress.

This, at any event, is one popular interpretation of Wellington's achievement.[1] It has tended to place him upon a pedestal so high that his human qualities and failings have been all but lost to view. Certain hagiographers have gone further still, and have almost seemed to suggest that Wellington's decisions were invariably correct, for the full and sufficient reason that his art of generalship was itself the definition of generalship. There are hints that his military *savoir faire* sprang fully formed from his adolescent brow, and that because he never lost a battle he must therefore never have made a mistake.

A formal portrait, by J. Hoppner, of Wellington fresh from his Indian triumphs.

The historian, however, must try to show how these apparently superhuman achievements could actually come to be performed by a sublunary being. Wellington was but a man, like many another, and he reached his ultimate stature as a general only through a lengthy and often painful process of trial and error. His rise to final glory was by no means uninterrupted or free from acrimony, and although he certainly did not lose any battle along the way, it is scarcely correct to claim that he was victorious in every campaign. His achievement was not that he was infallible, but rather that he knew how to weather his mistakes and make the best of a bad job. He had an enviable knack of equanimity which allowed him to sit out any crisis, thus giving his opponent plenty of time to make mistakes in turn.

This equanimity is well caught in the following portrait from G.R. Gleig's memoirs of the Pyrenees campaign:

> There was in his general aspect nothing indicative of a life spent in hardships and fatigues: nor any expression of care or anxiety in his countenance. On the contrary, his cheek, though bronzed with frequent exposure to the sun, had on it the ruddy hue of health, while a smile of satisfaction played about his mouth, and told, more plainly than words could have spoken, how perfectly he felt himself at his ease.[2]

Gleig here gives us a further clue to Wellington's success when he mentions his high physical health. Throughout his campaigns 'The Iron Duke' took great delight in riding and other outdoor pursuits, and his wiry frame possessed a notorious stamina which could outmatch that of even his strongest *aides*. When it came to paperwork his powers of concentration were no less fierce, and almost obsessional. His piercingly intense gaze – so vividly preserved for us in Goya's portrait – seemed to burn to the heart of any issue with inexorable precision. There was therefore nothing slack or lethargic about Wellington's equanimity: merely a carefully reasoned confidence that he had attended vigorously to everything which lay within his very considerable powers, so that there was nothing to be gained by worrying over the rest.

Wellington's energetic tranquillity was perhaps most marked on those occasions when he placed himself in the front line of the fighting. Where a serious crisis threatened, he would not hesitate to go forward to the place of danger and direct the battle with a cool but inspired eye. This was a very risky business, and he had horses killed beneath him. On at least two occasions he was hit by spent musket balls, while at other times he had narrow escapes from enemy cavalry and even from cannon shots aimed specifically at him. Contrary to popular belief, however, he did not like to expose himself without good reason, and was critical of generals who did so. Of Sir John Hope he had the following to say:

> We shall lose him if he continues to expose himself to fire as he did in those last three days: indeed his escape has been wonderful. He places himself among the sharp-shooters, without (as they do) sheltering himself from the enemy's fire. This will not answer: and I hope that his friends will give him a hint of the subject. But it is a *delicate* subject.[3]

Whether by luck or good judgement, Wellington himself managed to survive a remarkably long spell of active service. He took part in at least sixteen campaigns within the short span of twenty years, roaming widely around the globe from Brussels to Calcutta and from Copenhagen to Madrid. No other senior British commander in that era saw as much service as he did, and all too many succumbed to the rigours of campaigning. Abercrombie, Moore, Le Marchant, Craufurd, Picton, Packenham, Stevenson and James Stuart all bought their glory with their lives, being carried off by the enemy's shot or by the fatal diseases which always stalked in the train of an army in the field. Many another British officer was invalided home or lost his faculties under the strains and shocks of protracted warfare – but not so Wellington: he rode lightly through every campaign to enjoy both a successful second career and a ripe old age.

The youthful Wellington as Lieutenant Colonel of the 33rd Foot, by J. Hoppner.

Perhaps the secret of Wellington's robust powers of survival lay in his youthfulness and his very rapid promotion – by purchase and influence – to high rank. He was privileged to have tasted the potent elixir of high command while still in the first bloom of adulthood, before his inner fire could be dampened by a tedious garrison life in a subordinate role. Although he was first commissioned in 1787, he saw no more than ten months' regimental service before being transferred to a staff posting. Then in 1793, at the tender age of twenty-four, he was given a regiment of his own – the 33rd Foot. Within a year he was leading these troops on active service in the

Netherlands, and within six years he had taken up a major independent command in the Indian province of Mysore. His final campaign – once again in the Netherlands – was completed before he had reached his forty-seventh birthday.

In common with many of the French generals of his day, albeit for very different reasons, Wellington was thus vouchsafed an opportunity to demonstrate the enormous energies which youthful talent can bring to the command of armies. He had the ability to get things done, and as much in the administrative sphere as on the battlefield. It was in public administration, indeed, that he had received his true apprenticeship as an officer, between 1788 and 1793. For five years he had served as an *aide de camp* to the Lord Lieutenant of Ireland, and in the process he had gained an impressive understanding of the political and financial universe. When he eventually resumed his regimental career in 1793, therefore, Wellington found that he was in many ways more at home with the duties of a general than with those of a subaltern.

We tend to imagine Wellington as a commander in the field – a 'man on horseback' and a man of action. Paradoxically, however, his success probably depended more on the time he spent behind a desk than it did on his life outdoors. It was by dint of long hours of preparation and letter writing that he was able to come to grips with all aspects of the military problems which he confronted. When he entered a campaign he would go to considerable pains to inform himself as much as possible about the topography, the history and the politics of the theatre of war. He would read deeply into the subject and 'open a correspondence' with local informants on both sides of the enemy's lines. In Napoleonic times the collection of intelligence was a personal matter for any commander in chief, since in the absence of regular intelligence services he would often have to concern himself with it directly. Efficiency in this task could be quite as important as efficiency in logistics or in the issue of orders and other information to one's own forces. Wellington gave a great deal of attention to all of them.

He was an insatiable correspondent. His letters are as extensive in their volume as they are meticulous in their attention to detail. The style is pellucid, and reveals the full clarity and simplicity of the author's thoughts. They were not written without a considerable mental effort, however, and we have an impression that Wellington spent a great deal of his time thinking deeply about them. The inner tranquillity which he derived from mastery of his profession was hence achieved only by dint of long cogitation and analysis. On many occasions he would appear to be totally preoccupied and distant. He could display the brooding taciturnity – and even the shyness – of a scholar wrestling internally with some complex abstract problem. Mrs Shelly once remarked that 'He seldom speaks until he is well acquainted', and even with his close associates his customary approachability could sometimes wear thin. When his train of thought finally arrived at its destination

The Waterloo Gallery at Apsley House as it was for Wellington's annual banquets to commemorate the battle. On Waterloo day 1983 it was the scene of the *Wellington-Commander* Seminar.

he would happily set all care aside and indulge with gusto in light-hearted repartee: but until that point was reached some of his social graces might temporarily be suspended.

The public likes its heroes to have decisive temperaments. A problem is posed; the great man takes it in at a glance; finally he snaps out a miraculously accurate and effective decision. This is how we would all like to be, and we are more than ready to believe that it is how someone with Wellington's record actually was. We read of the decision to attack at Salamanca which he took, according to the legend, while he was half through chewing a chicken leg. We read of his instant identification of the uncharted fords at Assaye, or of his inspired improvisations at Waterloo. All this helps us to think of him as a man of quick decision. Yet on many occasions we find him racked with doubt and unable to reach a conclusion. In fact this was never more true than at Salamanca itself, where for days and weeks before his decisive stroke he had been agonising over the strategic gamble which was in prospect.

The very breadth of Wellington's horizon exacted a deeper analysis from him than would have seemed necessary to a shallower man. A very great deal of his time was therefore absorbed in thinking, sifting information, and in consultation with his staff. For example it is thought that both Beresford, the commander of the Portuguese army, and Murray, Wellington's indispensable Quartermaster General, at various times dissuaded him from some of his more risky initiatives and convinced him that he should leave a number of battles unfought. When it came to a sudden crisis Wellington could certainly rise magnificently to the occasion – but for much of the day-by-day direction of the army he liked to give himself plenty of time to make up his mind.

Wellington's air of scholarly detachment was doubtless reinforced by the patrician *hauteur* of his breeding and by his lack of regimental experience. He had scarcely known the intimate symbiosis with colleagues and subordinates which springs naturally from the command of a platoon or a company. Instead, he had a tendency to speak *de haut en bas*, without the softening mediation of what we would today call a 'public relations instinct'. Although he was personally very courteous and civil, he somehow failed to project these qualities into his public dealings. Try as he might, he often failed to explain his decisions to subordinates, often omitted to give credit where it was due, and often unknowingly gave offence. When his men showed signs of slackness he appeared to hector them, and when they performed their duty efficiently he seemed to take them for granted. He has gained notoriety for a number of unfortunate remarks about the British soldier – 'the scum of the earth' and so on – but his private letters are even more liberally sprinkled with criticisms of the British officer.

Wellington seemed unable to avoid controversy with other officers. This was an age in which the code of military etiquette was even more unfath-

Hillingford's dramatic Victorian evocation of Wellington encouraging a square at Waterloo. When the French cavalry came close both he and the supporting artillerymen would retire to the centre of the square.

General Sir George Murray GCB, the indispensable Chief of Staff in the Peninsula and the nearest anyone ever came to becoming Wellington's 'collaborator'.

omable and severe than usual, and in which offence was easily taken. Acrimony, litigation and even duelling were often the results of trifling perceived slights, particularly when precedence or promotion were involved. At Seringapatam it was Major-General Baird who felt that Wellington was being given unduly hasty preferment, and for several years there was a spasmodic vendetta between the two men. Later in his career Wellington was frequently to cause enormous resentment among his subordinates by what they saw as his unfair allocations of praise and blame in his despatches. Indeed, we find that during the Peninsular War he was at the centre of a furious dispute with his officers almost regularly once a year. In 1808 he had to undergo a lengthy court of Inquiry for his part in signing the Convention of Cintra with the defeated French army. The next year he was faced by factions of back-biters or 'Croakers' who criticised his plans for the defence of Portugal as over-optimistic. The Croakers gained a new lease of life in 1811 when they called for more decisive offensive operations, and in the ignominious retreat from Burgos in 1812 they held a veritable field day. Paradoxically some of the worst cases of croaking came in the sombre aftermath of victory, as after Vitoria in 1813 or Waterloo two years later. Each of these battles temporarily ruined the army which won it, and led to some very sour exchanges between Wellington and his officers. His celebrated refusal to write the history of Waterloo, indeed, stemmed from his consciousness of the many dishonourable incidents which the battle had provoked. Even five months after the event there was at least one officer still

Sir David Baird triumphant at Seringapatam. He was outraged that Wellington, who had been very junior during the campaign, should then be promoted above his head to command the newly-conquered provinces.

Captain Ramsey RHA won fame at Fuentes de Oñoro for extracting his guns from the very midst of an enemy cavalry charge – but he was later to be mortified by Wellington's harsh tongue.

trying to prove that his desertion of the colours had been because he was stunned, and not from cowardice. In this case Wellington accepted the story, but he drily remarked that 'Many a brave man, and I believe even some very great men, have been found a little terrified by such a battle as that ...'[4]

No public figure can avoid controversy, and none can afford to admit to too many mistakes. Self-justification in the face of malicious factions is almost inseparable from high office, and we should not perhaps find anything particularly exceptional in Wellington's record. We do have a feeling, nevertheless, that he somehow attracted rather more than his fair share of this sort of thing, and that his own abrasive character lay at the bottom of it all. He was respected for his many skills, admired for his achievements – but he was scarcely loved for his techniques of man-management. His soldiers liked to see him directing their battles and would cheer 'Douro! Douro!' when he made an appearance – but they did not at all like to hear what he thought of them.

We should not forget that Wellington could be a ferocious commander even by the standards of a ferocious profession in a ferocious age. He did not habitually apply punishments as freely as many imagine, but if he did see the need for an example to be made he would hang or flog his soldiers quite as readily as the next man. With his subordinates he insisted on the strictest observance of 'duty' and, as we have already seen, he could mortify even his closest associates by his criticisms. When it came to his allies he was often utterly contemptuous, certainly in private, and after the Nivelle battle he had no compunction about dismissing his undisciplined Spanish units from the campaign. At the battle of Argaum he did not even hesitate to attack his theoretical ally, the Maharajah Daulat Rao Sindhia, the moment it looked as though the latter had broken his treaty.

It was during his time in India, in fact, that Wellington was at his most ferocious. The restraints which applied to European warfare did not have the same force on the sub-continent, where it was axiomatic that a display of savagery could impress a hesitant population far more profoundly than any number of civilised niceties. Thus it was a common practice for Indian rulers who were defeated in battle to be executed for their pains, and at least three of Wellington's major adversaries suffered this fate. The strategy of 'scorched earth' was also well known in India, and Wellington did not underestimate its value. In 1810 he was to apply this cruel policy to Portugal, as his preferred means of saving that country from the French. In this respect, alas, he does not turn out to have been morally greatly superior to Ludendorff and Sherman after all.

By the same token it is difficult to know what to make of Wellington's orders for the siege of Pamplona in 1813. On this occasion he told his Spanish subordinate 'You may shoot the governor and his officers, and decimate the rank and file' – which was a suggestion quite contrary to 'the laws of war' as they were understood at that time. It was a threat which was never carried out, and was probably intended as no more than bluster to add urgency to the protracted negotiations for the city's surrender. As an integral part of Wellington's published records, none the less, it is not a passage which does him credit.

There is even a suspicion that Wellington may have been guilty of launching wars of aggression. In 1798 his elder brother Richard became Governor General of India and initiated a new policy of territorial expansion. Wellington (or Arthur Wesley as he had been up to then)[5] soon found himself

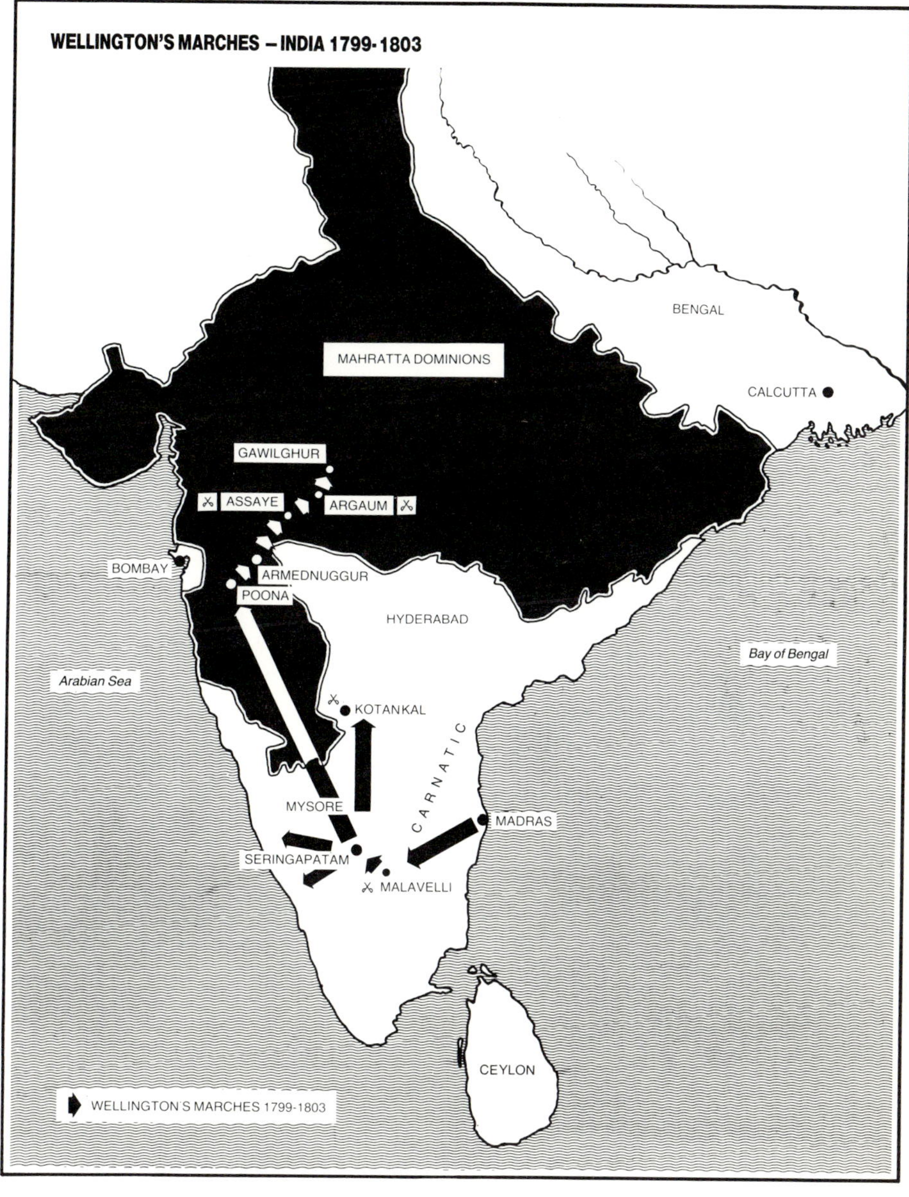

holding a series of independent commands on the very frontiers of the area under British control. Far from the government in Calcutta, he was responsible for making many of the important political decisions and conducting the key negotiations with troublesome local princelings. Whoever may have had the right of it in these murky and convoluted transactions, the end result was usually war and a rapid British victory. By 1804 the East India Company held sway throughout the interior of the sub-continent, whereas previously it had been confined to a few coastal provinces around the margins. This era in Wellington's life therefore reveals some striking parallels with Napoleon's early imperialistic escapades, and it has rarely been scrutinised critically by deferential Anglo-Saxon biographers.

In India Wellington quickly revealed not only his practical ruthlessness, but also his magnificent skill in organising military supplies. It is undeniable that he was a logistician *par excellence*, and he repeatedly overturned accepted wisdoms by the speed with which he could bring together a moving bazaar – actually a sort of free-enterprise 'rolling magazine' – to keep his forces fed while they operated far from their base. His campaigns were therefore notable for their range and cross-country mobility, even in near-desert conditions. Wellington became expert in taking the war to the

The ferocity of Indian warfare – a cavalry clash at Assaye.

enemy's camp and running him to earth in territory which had conventionally been thought inaccessible.

These same logistic and organisational skills were later deployed in Spain, which to some extent resembled India by virtue of its difficulties of supply. In this case Wellington had to contend with all the severe shortages of transport which usually attended British expeditions overseas, so once again he had to improvise much of his logistic infrastructure on the spot. Once he had made it work, however, this system became a vital trump card in Wellington's hands. It gave him great advantages over the French who, at least until Marmont's reforms in 1812, relied upon 'locust methods' for their foraging. Their supply arrangements lacked the precision, predictability and regularity of Wellington's, which meant that their operations tended to suffer from a relative fragility and inflexibility.

This contrast between British efficiency and French fragility is all the more striking since in so many other campaigns of the Napoleonic era there was a precisely opposite balance. Numerous were the administratively chaotic British landings at unlikely points around the European coastline which the French were able to brush disdainfully aside. Wellington himself had seen this happen in the Netherlands in 1794, and it continued to happen

The movement of men, horses and stores was of paramount importance to Wellington's campaigns. This picture shows the crossing of the Bidassoa in 1813.

This patriotic portrayal of the 'ease' of amphibious assault fails to show the appalling difficulties which the British habitually faced when they threw badly-supported expeditionary forces ashore on the hostile European coasts.

elsewhere while the Peninsular War was itself in progress. It happened on a considerable scale at Walcheren in 1809 and it happened once again at Tarragona in 1813. If it were not for Wellington's rather unusual series of successes with 'his' army, we would certainly be entitled to suppose that the British under George III were almost irredeemably inept in the art of warfare on land. What Wellington managed to do, however, and what so many of his contemporaries failed to do, was to persuade the troops under his command to perform with something approaching the efficiency which was theoretically expected of them. He converted an essentially ramshackle and amateurish organisation into a true army, complete with all necessary ancillary services as well as the vital spirit of professional self-confidence which had hitherto been missing. This change in the nature of the army was by no means easy to achieve, nor was it ever finally completed to the full satisfaction of its author. Right to the end Wellington continued to complain of slackness among the junior officers, plundering and other irregularities among the troops, recklessness among the cavalry and lack of

Not even 'Daddy' Hill – one of Wellington's most effective and active subordinates – was given total trust by the 'Iron Duke'.

punctuality in the commissariat. Not even his most senior officers managed to live up to all his high standards of staff competence, and he repeatedly grumbled that 'I am obliged to be everywhere, and if absent from any operation, something goes wrong.'[6] Thus Marshal Beresford, Wellington's right hand man and the creator of the Portuguese army, was almost beaten at Albuera in 1811 and lost far more casualties than he ought. Lieutenant General Hill, the brilliant victor of raids like Arroyomolinos in 1811 or Almaraz in 1812, failed to keep in touch with events at Maya in 1813 and hence contributed to a potential disaster in the Pyrenees which was finally averted by only the narrowest of margins. There was no one, it seemed, whom Wellington could ultimately trust to be consistently efficient. He felt that he had to supervise any important business in person.

Like Napoleon, Wellington was in many ways a 'one man band'. He was not very good at delegation, or at training a staff which could function smoothly in his absence. He left no institutions behind him which could compare with the great Prussian General Staff, and after Toulouse the

Peninsular army which he had built up so carefully was almost immediately dismantled. In the Hundred Days Wellington had to start the work of army-building almost from scratch.

The fact remains, nevertheless, that wherever he was present in person an army would be built. Even with the least promising material, such as the 'second battalions and other sweepings' of 1809, Wellington possessed a remarkable gift for imposing regularity and order. There were many parts of the British military machine which not even he could do anything about – for example it was only in 1813 that he started to get effective control over the appointment of his officers – yet he did not become discouraged or abandon the case as hopeless. As much as anything, it was due to his dogged optimism that he was prepared to fight his way through the bureaucratic miasma for so long. There seemed to be few good grounds for hoping that a British force could ever become truly efficient, and on many occasions he was let down. Despite repeated disappointments, however, he persisted and reached a result which, although far short of perfect, could at least pass muster as an army.

There is no doubt that much of Wellington's success derived from his sanguine calm and reasoned energy; his youth and his administrative skills. Above all it came from his powers as an army-builder and an army-feeder. These qualities set him high above all too many of his contemporaries, yet we should nevertheless remember that it is not by these things that the art of generalship is traditionally judged. Generalship is normally assessed rather by the manner in which armies are manoeuvered and directed in action. If we wish for a complete picture of Wellington's art of command it is to his specific operations and style of fighting that we must now turn.

In India the British regiments were normally very heavily outnumbered by their enemies and could scarcely hope to win 'set-piece' or deliberate battles. If an enemy army was poised and ready, its numerical superiority could be employed to its fullest effect. The British therefore saw that the art of victory ought to consist in throwing a cumbersome enemy off balance by a sudden and violent attack from an unexpected direction. Such an offensive, even if it were delivered by very few troops, could disrupt an enemy's line, throw him into confusion and neutralise all his advantages of numbers.

On his arrival in Madras immediately after his military apprenticeship in Dublin and Holland, Wellington was quick to absorb these principles of sepoy warfare. Indeed, we may even suggest that they became totally fundamental to his entire approach to military operations. In the Seringapatam campaign he saw and appreciated the power of a strategic offensive at first hand, even though his first tactical action at Malavelli was a defensive skirmish and his second, at Sultanpetah Tope, was an excessively daring night attack. On this occasion his troops lost cohesion in the darkness and were repulsed. After this galling setback he was never again anxious to fight at night, although in other respects his ardour for the attack remained undimmed.

When Wellington became commander of Mysore after the siege of Seringapatam, he found himself well placed to develop a thorough-going system of offensive operations. His expeditions became ever bolder and ever more mobile. In every case, moreover, the strategic offensive was topped out by an opportunist tactical assault. This happened in open battle at Manoli and Kotankal in 1800, and it happened in the sieges of Dummul in the same year, Arrakerry a year later and then, most notably, Armednuggur and Gawilghur in 1803. Wellington's Indian sieges showed few of the refinements of a scientific approach '*en règle*', and were usually settled by an incautious headlong rush by a handful of very determined infantry.

The real masterpieces of Wellington's Indian technique were perhaps his two large battles against the Mahrattas – Assaye and Argaum. Both of them were cast in the same mould, since on both occasions Wellington stumbled across the enemy army at the end of a tiring march, made a rapid personal reconnaissance and then determined that an immediate attack was preferable to an overnight delay. On both occasions he brought up his troops in echelons to one flank in a manner very reminiscent of Frederick the Great's celebrated 'oblique order'. Like Frederick, he was thus able to concentrate

The storming of Gawilghur, 1803, showing the lightness of the artillery preparation and the absence of formal siegeworks.

a powerful spearhead against a single point in the opposing line. In both battles – especially Assaye – there was some hard fighting and some errors by subordinate commanders; but in both cases the British bayonet was ultimately triumphant. Enormously strong but tactically un-manoeuverable enemy forces were routed by a few thousand Europeans.

Four years after Argaum, Wellington was again applying these robust tactical principles in battle. At Köge near Copenhagen he charged the numerically superior Danish militia in an echelon of battalions, and turned them about after a single volley. Although fought in Northern Europe, this battle was in many ways entirely 'Indian' in its structure and it must be admitted that the enemy can have ranked scarcely higher on the scale of military competence than the Mahrattas themselves. The chief difference from Wellington's Indian operations was perhaps that on this occasion he commanded only a brigade – a considerable step down from his former oriental glory. The particular brigade in question, however, was later to grow into the celebrated Light Division of the Peninsular War. These troops were already steeped in the skills of skirmishing and outpost duty which were to be so important in Portugal and Spain, and Wellington's early association with them must have been a considerable influence on him as he prepared himself for the greater conflicts that were soon to come.

When he went to Portugal in 1808 Wellington was aware that he was at last entering 'the big league' of modern warfare. He had already seen the French army in action during the Dutch campaign of 1793–4, and its reputation since then had done nothing but increase. Under Napoleon the French had conquered almost the whole of Europe, gaining regularity and confidence as they went. Wellington could not afford to underestimate them, but neither could he see any reason to change his style of fighting. His analysis of the French victories led him to the view that they stemmed more from disorganisation and panic among the allies than from any particular cleverness on the part of the French themselves. The French might overwhelm Wellington by their numbers, he thought, but they would not be able to outmanœuvre him – 'First, because I am not afraid of them, as everyone else seems to be; and secondly, because (if all I hear about their system is true) I think it a false one against steady troops. I suspect all the continental armies are half-beaten before the battle begins. I at least will not be frightened beforehand.'[7]

When he landed at Mondego Bay, therefore, Wellington easily slipped into his normal style of offensive operations. He charged South towards Lisbon with his usual impetus, and knocked Delaborde's division out of its position near Roliça with scarcely a pause to draw breath. Admittedly Wellington had originally hoped to achieve this by flanking manœuvres rather than by a frontal assault, but the rash Colonel Lake of the 29th determined otherwise when he became unexpectedly embroiled with the enemy centre. After Roliça the British pressed on again and were about to make their final offensive against a numerically inferior enemy, under General Junot, when Junot moved forward and tried to seize the initiative by a sharp counter-attack at Vimeiro.

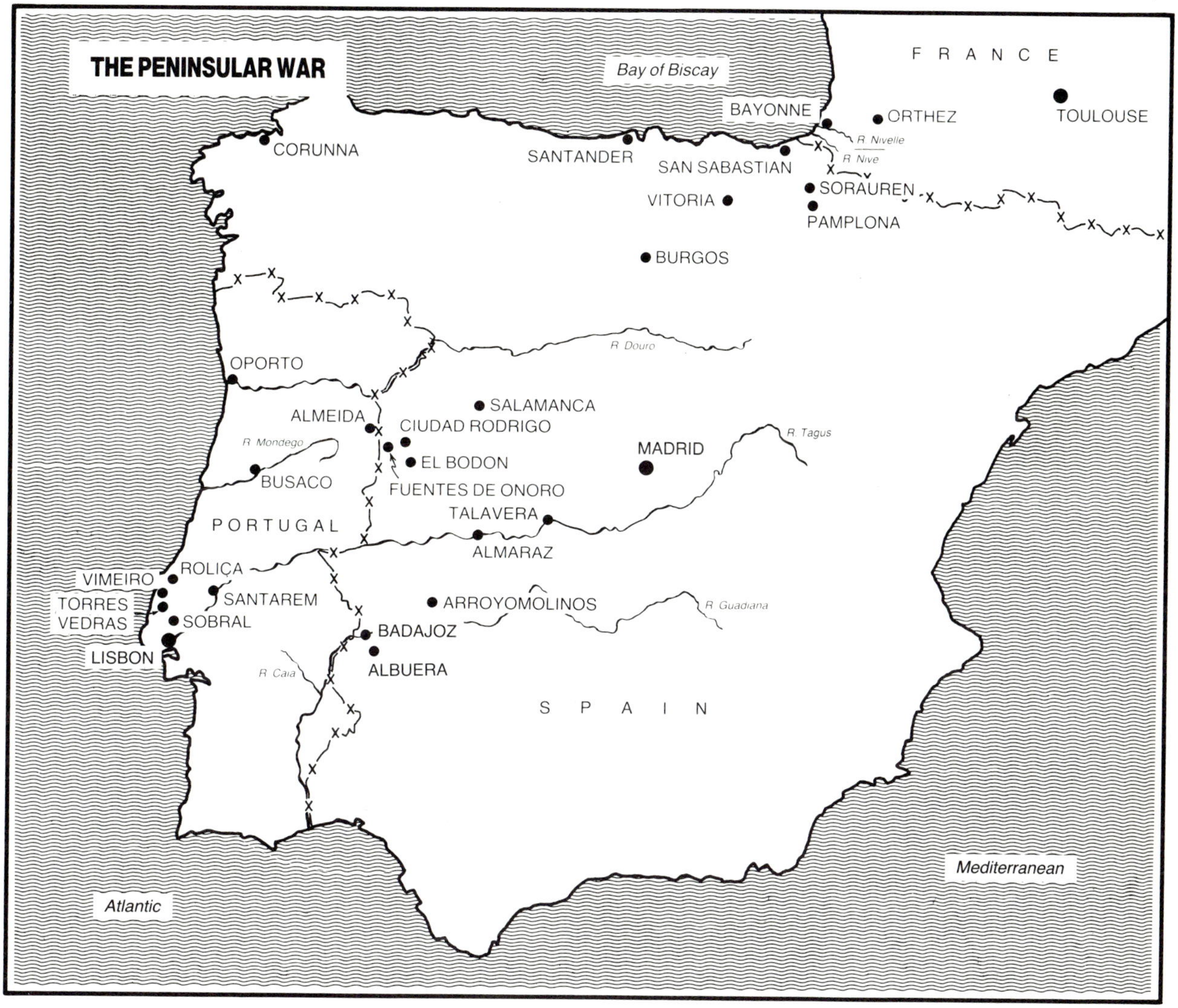

It speaks volumes for the difference in quality between the French and Wellington's previous opponents that Junot should have believed he could pull off a counter-attack against superior numbers. He commanded no shambling, unmanœuverable mob but a sophisticated veteran force accustomed to crushing every enemy who stood in its path. Indeed, it was only by a rapid change of front and some bold downhill charges that Wellington was able to ward off the danger. He defeated the French, in other words, only because he proved to be quite as manœuverable and flexible as they were. Had his footwork not been quite so quick he would doubtless have shared

LEFT: General Junot, the over-aggressive commander of the first French invasion of Portugal.

RIGHT: Sir John Moore, who did much to see the British Army through its dark years around 1800, and who drew off the French to Corunna in 1808–9, but who ruined his army and lost his own life in the attempt.

the ignominious fate suffered by so many other commanders who had tried to oppose the armies of Napoleon.

Wellington's instinct after Vimeiro was to make an immediate pursuit of the defeated foe, but he was restrained in this by the unwelcome arrival of an elderly superior officer who imposed a halt on operations. The French army was not annihilated as it might have been, but was eventually shipped back to France under the terms of the Convention of Cintra. Wellington went home to defend his role in the affair before a court of Inquiry, while Sir John Moore took over command of a heavily reinforced Peninsular Army.

Moore's orders forced him reluctantly to take the offensive and he carried the attack boldly into northern Spain, where he hoped to link hands with some of the Spanish armies which were still operating against the French. In this hope, however, he was disappointed. Napoleon reacted strongly and rapidly to the threat by making a powerful concentration of armies around the exposed British force. The Spanish were kept out of the reckoning, and it was only with the greatest difficulty that Moore was able to make good his escape to Corunna. He was killed in action there, although most of his troops managed to embark for home – albeit in a deplorably ragged and exhausted state. With his daring offensive Moore had been made to seriously overplay his hand, effectively wrecking the finest British expeditionary force to be sent overseas thus far during the Napoleonic era.

Wellington studied the Corunna campaign with great interest, and reached the intellectual conclusion that the French in Spain were too strong to be beaten easily. The Spanish armies were too badly co-ordinated, while the British were too weak to stand unsupported on the great plains in the heartland of the Peninsula. To this extent he agreed with the lesson drawn from Corunna by most other observers. Unlike most critics, however, Wellington also saw that the mountainous regions, especially in Portugal, did offer some excellent possibilities for defence and might perhaps be made strong enough to withstand the heaviest French attacks. Wellington thus conceived what he was later to call his 'cautious system', whereby Portugal would be garrisoned by British troops, the infant Portuguese army would be built up, and the French harassed from a position of safety. He realised that the Peninsular War would be a long haul, and would be decided by attrition rather than by the outcome of any one brilliant campaign.

In April 1809 the 'cautious system' was under consideration in Wellington's mind as he again landed in Portugal to take command of the British troops there. He certainly understood the theoretical logic of the cautious approach and he knew in particular that Portuguese defence must be his highest priority; but we have an impression that all his instincts were still craving for a renewal of the lightning offensive. The habit of a decade's campaigning could not easily be laid to one side. In the event, therefore, all caution was apparently thrown to the winds. Within three weeks of landing in Lisbon Wellington had marched north and evicted Marshal Soult from Oporto in a most hazardous but spectacularly successful operation. Within ten weeks he was on the road into the plains of Estremadura, full of confidence that with Spanish help he could crush the army corps of Marshal Victor and capture the glittering prize of Madrid itself. So far had he departed from his earlier analysis of Moore's mistakes that he seemed set fair to repeat every single one of them, almost down to the last detail.

It was at Talavera on 27th – 28th July that Wellington finally met Victor in battle, but it was in circumstances very different from those originally envisaged. Far from falling on an isolated French detachment with an overwhelmingly powerful allied army, Wellington found that by the time he could reach them the French had more than doubled their numbers. Delays in the allied timetable, mostly imposed by the Spanish general Cuesta and his dreadfully inefficient commissariat, had allowed Victor to be reinforced by Sebastiani's corps and King Joseph's reserve from Madrid. To make matters worse Wellington failed to get constructive co-operation from Cuesta in the tactical manœuvres, so that the French were permitted to concentrate their entire weight against the British contingent. What had been intended as an allied attack with a superiority of more than two to one against the French became a desperate defensive action in which there were more than two Frenchmen to each British soldier. For almost thirty-six hours Wellington held his ground under repeated assaults and by the end about 5,000 men – more than a quarter of his force – had been made casualty. 'Never was there such a murderous battle', said Wellington,[8] which was certainly true enough within his own personal experience.

In all his many adventures Wellington had never previously undergone any test so severe as this. Only at Vimeiro had he even been thrown onto the defensive, but on that occasion he had not suffered the destruction of major units nor had the enemy attacks persisted long beyond the initial onset. At the start of Talavera, by contrast, the British had several battalions severely mauled in the outposts, while at the crisis of the battle the centre of the main fighting line charged too far into the French reserves and was badly beaten. Wellington faced and mastered an excruciating crisis on the latter occasion, even though his own reserves had been practically exhausted. We can only wonder at his philosophical attitude in his after-action despatch, when he heaped praise on the Guards (who had behaved recklessly in the centre and had been routed) as well as on the Spanish (who had let him down on every possible occasion).

If Vimeiro had been a near run thing, Talavera was much, much nearer. The British were able to maintain their position only by the narrowest of margins, and were too badly mauled to contemplate any counter-stroke after the French assaults had been defeated. Wellington had originally hoped that the Spanish would be available for this phase of the action, but he was once again disappointed. Nor could any strategic benefits be drawn from the tactical victory, since the breakdown of supply imposed a hasty retreat to more abundant areas. The French also continued to draw together fresh contingents to counter the allied threat. At Almaraz Marshal Soult, with a very powerful corps, almost reached a position from which to bring Wellington to battle but was beaten to the post by a short head. At all events the British had no option but to cut their losses and scamper back to the shelter of Portugal before they were either cut off by their enemies or starved by their allies. This was indeed Moore's retreat all over again, and it left Wellington with no illusion about either the reliability of the Spanish or the striking power of his own force.

Whereas Corunna had persuaded Wellington's intellect that a 'cautious system' was the best policy for the British in Portugal, Talavera more than converted his instincts to the same view. The whole episode was so laden with disappointments and narrow escapes that it stamped a new prudence onto his hitherto recklessly aggressive style of operations. After Talavera Wellington at last started to believe that his army might be beaten unless it was very carefully husbanded, and for a short time he even seemed to think that an evacuation of the whole Peninsula would eventually be necessary.[9]

Despair was not a part of Wellington's character, however, and he soon threw himself into practical efforts to defend Portugal without putting the British force at risk. The Portuguese army was built up, the avenues of approach along the frontier were covered by outposts and the final fall-back positions at Torres Vedras were secretly constructed. The whole of Portugal was converted into a gigantic trap for the French, who were to be allowed free access into a countryside denuded of food supplies – but denied either a decisive battle or access to Lisbon and its essential harbour. With their 'locust methods' of foraging, the French would be invited to eat their way into the trap, but deprived of the wherewithal to eat their way out again. This was a very drastic measure designed to meet what was, after all, a very drastic crisis. It certainly represented the diametrical opposite to Wellington's customary style of mobile and decisive action, and it certainly hurt the Portuguese peasants very hard indeed.

With the benefit of hindsight we can perhaps fault Wellington for learning the bitter lessons of Talavera only too well. For more than two years he seemed to be even more cautious and circumspect than the case demanded, although it is also true that at this period there were heavier external pressures upon him than in the past. After the Walcheren *débâcle* there were no other British expeditionary forces in reserve, so Whitehall was more anxious than ever that the Peninsular army should survive intact. After Wagram, moreover, Napoleon was no longer tied down to his Eastern front, and could bring exceptionally large forces to bear upon Portugal.

The fact nevertheless remains that the French attack did not materialise until many months after Wellington had expected it. When it did come, furthermore, he let pass many excellent opportunities for destroying it in battle. Thus on Busaco ridge Wellington repulsed several massed attacks in a most convincing manner, but failed once again to finish the business with a decisive counter-stroke. Instead, he meekly allowed Massena to turn his flank and force the planned retreat to Torres Vedras. We are thus left with a certain feeling that Wellington was applying passivity almost as a system, and that he was slavishly following his pre-determined timetable regardless of the balance of advantage on the ground.

At Busaco it was at least true that the French enjoyed a numerical superiority over the Anglo-Portuguese army. As the winter wore on, how-

'One of the finest defensive positions in Europe' – the ridge at Busaco which Wellington was able to hold against all comers until his flank was turned.

ever, the odds gradually shifted against them. Unable either to eat or to advance through the lines of Torres Vedras, Massena's troops wilted away while Wellington was able to build up his own forces with reinforcements from Britain. In the early spring there were opportunities for a British offensive on favourable terms around Sobral and Santarem, but once again Wellington let them pass. He leapt into action only when the French had started to withdraw to Spain, and was not best pleased to find that they could show him a fairly clean pair of heels. There was no annihilation of Massena's army; no new Baylen. It survived to fight another day and its losses, although grievous, were quickly made good.

Wellington's fourth defensive battle came at Fuentes de Oñoro, when Massena returned to the charge only a month after he had regained his base in Spain, and before the British had completed their consolidation of Portugal. Unlike Busaco, the battle was a close shave, and Wellington felt that he had been lucky to avoid defeat at the hands of such an enterprising and manœuverable foe. On this occasion he decided against a counter-offensive, after the attacks had been warded off, both because the French remained too strong and because such a movement would require a concentration of force that might uncover the allied siege of Almeida.[10] Caution, in other words, remained the keynote.

Wellington's caution was also reflected in his measures to keep his casualties to a minimum. By his use of the ground and outposts in depth he was able to protect his main line from the enemy's fire and thereby make economies in manpower. In four days on an indifferent position at Fuentes he lost scarcely more men than he had in a morning at Busaco on the strongest position in Portugal; some 1,600 as against 1,200, or less than a third of the

The brook, running through the eastern part of Fuentes de Oñoro village, which marked 'no man's land' for much of the battle in 1811. Note the stout stone construction of the buildings.

casualties suffered at Talavera. At Fuentes there was also a sense of balance and control about the defence which had been missing in the hectic improvisations of Vimeiro and Talavera, no less than in the unadventurous straightforwardness of Busaco. Wellington by 1811 had finally perfected his art of defensive tactics and had assembled the technique which he was later to demonstrate with such effect at Waterloo. It was only unfortunate that he was absent from Albuera, ten days after Fuentes, when an uncharacteristically violent attack by Marshal Soult almost broke another allied defensive position, this one covering the siege of Badajoz. At Albuera there were some 6,000 allied casualties, which was about 600 more than Wellington had suffered at Talavera.

If Wellington's caution was at its strongest during this period, it would seem that his opponents were also themselves beginning to learn a little prudence of their own. They had been used to meeting shambling Spanish armies which collapsed with as much readiness as Wellington's Mahrattas had done in 1803; and like Wellington they had adopted a habit of careless *attaque à l'outrance*. At Vimeiro, Talavera, Busaco and now again at Fuentes and Albuera this system had nevertheless failed to produce the desired result, and French commanders were starting to perceive that the Anglo-Portuguese war machine was made of considerably sterner stuff than the Spanish. In the summer of 1811, therefore, we have an intriguing spectacle of two opposed armies which were each, to all intents and purposes, scared of the other. On a number of occasions there were confrontations which did not lead to battles because neither side felt strong enough to force the issue. On the Caia, near Badajoz, Marmont and Soult effected a junction of 60,000 men against Wellington's 44,000, but believed that his force was actually

Marshal Marmont, the battery commander at Marengo who had risen to the command of armies by 1811. He was badly defeated by Wellington at Salamanca in 1812, and wounded into the bargain.

more numerous, and went home. Shortly after this Marmont made a new approach on the northern corridor around Ciudad Rodrigo, and fought a skirmish at El Bodon. The odds were very similar to those of the Caia confrontation, but once again Marmont failed to get the battle he needed.

For Wellington 1811 must have been a frustrating year since, despite his successes against Massena, and despite his victorious 'non battles' against Marmont and Soult, he was ultimately unable to score any major triumph. There were still great French fortresses at the gates of Portugal, and great French armies lurking behind them. Wellington felt that he could launch small scale raids into Spain, such as Hill's very successful surprise and destruction of a French brigade at Arroyomolinos, but that larger operations were still beyond his power. He was also very conscious of the logistic void which existed all around the Portuguese frontiers, acting as a severe limitation to the size of forces that could be kept in the field. 'We cannot venture to undertake any thing with a small body', he wrote, 'and a large body would starve'.[11]

At the start of 1812 Wellington did at least feel that he could carry through quick assaults on the frontier fortresses of Ciudad Rodrigo and Badajoz. As he had in his Indian sieges, he relied more on a rapid and risky attack than the full scientific but protracted methods of the engineer. In both cases he was successful, although the 'butcher's bill' was extremely high – some 5,900 allied casualties in the two operations, four fifths of them

BELOW: A panorama of the siege of Badajoz by the British and Portuguese, 1812.

RIGHT TOP: Badajoz today – the ramparts still hold an aura of menace.

RIGHT BOTTOM: The Badajoz ramparts and citadel photographed from the viewpoint used by the artist in the panorama below.

Artist's impression of the storming of Badajoz – an action which in fact took place in the dark.

at Badajoz. On both occasions there was also an undisciplined sack following the storming of the breaches, and Wellington must have reflected that many more such victories would be the ruin of his army.

After the capture of Badajoz the cautious system of manœuvre and counter-manœuvre was resumed along the frontier, although with the fortresses secure behind him Wellington could now afford to venture rather further into Spain than in the previous year. He also knew that French reinforcements were being channelled away into the Russian campaign, so some of his lost boldness could gradually be retrieved. On 26th May he even went so far as to declare – for the first time since the Talavera campaign – that he was actively seeking to bring the enemy to battle: 'The certainty of the loss in every action, and the risk which always attends such an operation, ought not, therefore, in my opinion, to prevent its being tried at present. I am not insensible to these losses and risks, nor am I blind to the disadvantages under which I shall undertake this operation . . .'[12]

In the event, however, it was the difficulties and dangers which seem to have gained the upper hand, and in a series of almost bloodless confrontations around Salamanca we see once again the cautious Wellington refusing to be drawn. He was impressed by the unexpected size and manœuverability of Marmont's army, and was apprehensive for the security of his own line of communications. On 21st July Wellington wrote that 'I have therefore determined ... not to fight an action, unless under very advantageous circumstances, or it should become absolutely necessary'.[13] Instead of taking a bold offensive, in fact, he had decided to pack his bags and return, once again, to Portugal. As after Vimeiro, Talavera and Fuentes, it seemed as though an enterprise which had started boldly was about to lead, yet again, to an inconclusive and frustrating result.

This period of Wellington's career gives us a fascinating picture of a man who is hopelessly torn between his natural instinct for decisive action and his painfully acquired understanding of the risks. He is no longer the reckless gambler of Assaye, but neither is he entirely the timid actuary of Torres Vedras. Instead, he is visibly wrestling to find some middle course by which he can win the triumph which has eluded him for so long, without falling into the near disaster of some new Corunna or Talavera. Such an ideal middle course could not be found, however, and Wellington was eventually forced to the uncomfortable realisation that if he wanted to reap any positive result from this campaign he had no alternative but to stake his all. It was thus in a mood close to desperation that on the morning of 22nd July he watched Marmont inexorably turning his flank and forcing him ever nearer to the final admission of failure.[14] For three years Wellington had been held unwillingly in check by these contemptible French combinations, and yet here he was once again being compelled to submit before them. To a man whose spectacular early career had promised so much – who had certainly been a second Clive, and perhaps even a second Bonaparte – this final ignominy suddenly seemed to be insupportable. Taking his courage in both hands, and reminding us vividly of the man of Assaye, he seized upon the first slight mistake which he detected in the French deployment. He launched his whole army impatiently forward into the sort of wild charge that had by this time been all but forgotten in the sedate military transactions of the Peninsula. Fortunately it surprised the French rather more than it surprised Wellington's own associates, and led to almost complete victory. Marmont was wounded and his army put to flight with stupendous losses. Here at last was the battle of annihilation which had not been seen since Baylen! Here at last was a British commander who had determined no longer to be overawed!

Wellington in triumph accepts the keys of Madrid, 1812.

In the wake of the battle of Salamanca Wellington finally reached Madrid – the succulent prize which had seemed so unattainable during all the cautious years of frustration. At the height of this triumph, however, he most incautiously made a division of his army which led him , as at Talavera, to overstretch his resources. Whether from overconfidence in his newly recovered audacity, or from his ingrained underestimation of the difficulties of fortress warfare, he was tempted north with the less robust half of his army to undertake a most ill-considered siege of Burgos. In the absence of adequate equipment, he launched several reckless assaults which failed to

LEFT TOP: An early print of the city and cathedral of Salamanca in 1812, with French prisoners marching into captivity following Wellington's victory.

LEFT BOTTOM: R. Simkin, a late Victorian artist, has exploited the Salamanca city skyline as a background for his imaginative interpretation of the battle. In fact the fighting took place some miles away from, and out of sight of, the city.

BELOW: The French 'Arapiles' on the actual field of Salamanca, in 1963.

take the citadel before the French could assemble an army of relief. At the end of the season Wellington was therefore compelled to abandon his siege and take the now familiar *via dolorosa* back into Portugal. It was a bitter reversal of fortune, and the third time since 1808 that a British army had ventured too far into the Spanish heartlands for its safety. There were scenes during the retreat which brought back vivid memories of the retreat to Corunna, and there were some painful exchanges between Wellington and his officers. This was by no means the way he had intended the year to end, and it must have powerfully reinforced his desire to exact his revenge in 1813.

During the winter the war went into abeyance and Wellington found a rare spell of leisure in which to reflect upon all that had happened in his most eventful year so far. He must have seen his own lack of decision around Salamanca, and his uncertain touch at Burgos, as symptoms of the very ambiguous balance of power in the Peninsula at this time. A cautious system was no longer unavoidable, and yet a daring offensive was not yet the obvious course. 1812 marked the turning of the tide of war, with neither the ebb nor the flow in a clear ascendency. It also marked the turning point in Wellington's personal development as a general, since it finally showed

him that even in the 'big league' of warfare against large French armies he could still apply his old recklessness, when appropriate, and get away with it. At Salamanca he had made an attack which he would have considered criminal a year earlier – but he had won. At Burgos he had repeated all the mistakes of Talavera and Corunna – yet he had survived. At last he could begin to put his experience at Talavera into its balanced perspective and realise that the dangers of such adventures, although great, were actually less than mortal. He may have realised, perhaps, that the unscathed victor of Assaye, Vimeiro and Oporto had originally reacted too strongly to his first serious check, and had swung too far from a policy of total aggression to one of total caution.

The whole of the 'cautious system' after Talavera had been based upon an absolute – the idea that under no circumstances should the precious Anglo-Portuguese army hazard its existence by initiating a battle. It could by all means stand in line on strong positions covering vital points, challenging the French to attack or not as the mood might strike them; but it should on no account itself take the great gamble of launching an offensive, no matter how sorely it might be tempted. In 1812 this system had started to break down as Wellington became impatient and found, to his great surprise and pleasure, that the rigidities of the 'cautious system' could safely be relaxed after all. The defensive reflexes branded upon him at Talavera were no longer his prison. He was free once more to 'get into Fortune's way',[15] and was now poised to draw from the ashes of Burgos a Phoenix of unparallelled military glory.

The campaign of 1813 was conceived as an offensive at both the strategic and tactical levels. It was no unplanned improvisation like Salamanca, Madrid or Burgos, but a deliberate and highly orchestrated seizure of the initiative right across the board. By a series of wide left-flanking sweeps the enemy was pushed back to the plain of Vitoria where his position – again by wide-flanking movements – was turned and practically encircled. He was forced to flee in confusion, leaving both his artillery and the fabulous booty of his entire sojourn in Spain to the gleeful attentions of the British serviceman at play.

Vitoria possessed a quality of finality which had somehow been absent from all of Wellington's earlier contests. It was the end of little King Joseph in Spain; the end of all the fears which had stalked in Wellington's shadow for four long years and, especially, the end of the French army as a credible bogeyman. Vitoria acted as a tonic to the embattled sovereigns of Eastern Europe; it inspired Beethoven's quill no less than it unlocked the gratitude of the British government. It was a symbol of triumph, even though allied casualties had again exceeded the ominous total of 5,000 which had caused so much remorse at Talavera, Albuera, Badajoz, and even Salamanca itself. Vitoria was yet another bloodbath – but this time it somehow did not seem to matter. With a whoop and a cheer the unstoppable Peninsular army had

Goya's equestrian portrait of Wellington, executed in 1812. This painting was hastily superimposed on a half-finished canvas showing either Joseph Bonaparte or Godoy, both of whom were forced to flee Madrid as a result of the battle of Salamanca.

ABOVE: 'With a whoop and a cheer' the Peninsular army defeats the French at Vitoria and liberates the untold riches in King Joseph's baggage train.

TOP RIGHT: Pamplona, showing the cathedral atop the fortified rocky cliffs.

BOTTOM LEFT: The battlefield of Sorauren, showing the steep slope up which the French had to advance to reach the allied line.

BOTTOM RIGHT: The near-vertical hillside which was successfully stormed by Wellington's troops towards the end of the battle of Sorauren.

put the finishing touches to both its formula for victory and its legend of success. Wellington had finally made his name.

What followed was admittedly a shade less glorious, since the indiscipline of pillage conspired with a somewhat uncertain direction of the pursuit to delay the arrival of the allies along the French frontier. When they did arrive they sat down to reduce the fortresses of Pamplona and San Sebastian, but were almost immediately taken by surprise in an energetic counter-stroke by Marshal Soult. Wellington's eyes had been concentrated on San Sebastian and the coast road while the French contrived to push back his outposts on the inland mountain passes. Only a rather hectic realignment of the reserves allowed a defence to be established at Sorauren, although the line was eventually held and the threat to Pamplona removed. At the end of the battle of Sorauren we even see Wellington ordering a frontal attack against an almost vertical mountainside – 'a position which is one of the strongest and most difficult of access that I have yet seen occupied by troops', as he put it.[16] If there remained any doubt that his power of offensive action had returned in full, this bold assault ought surely to have dispelled it.

Sorauren was fought at the end of July, but it was not until the following February that Wellington had shaken himself fully clear of the Pyrenees and the region of Bayonne. The critic may perhaps be entitled to carp at this delay and suggest that the sword of Vitoria had lost some of its sharpness. Many critics did indeed make this complaint at the time, but Wellington replied that he was anxious that everything in France should be done with regularity and order. If he had irrupted into the plains prematurely he would have lacked the money he needed to buy provisions, and would thus have alienated the populace by the necessity of plunder. He also had to bring forward his line of communication and reduce the enemy fortresses on his rear – a task which took considerably longer than he had originally foreseen. Only in November was he ready to resume the offensive, and the remarkable thing was that he then cut through some of the strongest mountain defences in Europe without a setback. Each of his bounds forward may have been tightly controlled and limited in range, but each one achieved total success in very difficult and extensively fortified country. It was only unfortunate for the general impetus of the campaign that the onset of winter imposed a halt before Bayonne during the first six weeks of 1814.

When operations were eventually re-started they came as thick and fast as anyone could wish. This was the true 'break-out and pursuit' phase which followed the difficult close battle in the mountains. It showed Wellington on his deadliest form, making strategic outflanking movements and tactical assaults with equal rapidity and *panache*. At Orthez he was back to his old habit of making a flank attack in echelons against an apparently formidable position, and breaking it with relative ease. At Toulouse he conducted an even more dangerous and costly flank attack against a range of strongly fortified hills. There was almost a disaster, but by this time the French had received such a beating that they were unable to make the best of their position and collapsed just before news came through of Napoleon's abdication. As Wellington had clearly foreseen, it was only Napoleon and his army which had felt any enthusiasm for continuing the war, and the moderation of the British towards the French population helped to ensure a smooth transfer of power once 'the ogre' had gone.

So ended the Peninsular War, which was by far the most important contribution made by the British Army to the downfall of Napoleon. For seven years it had been a running sore for the French which could have been healed only if every allied field army in Spain and Portugal had been destroyed. On a number of occasions the French had come close to achieving this objective, but it was usually Wellington who had prevented them. After the shock of Talavera he had perhaps fulfilled this task with rather less brilliance and dash than might have been expected of him; but he had fulfilled it nonetheless. Many another would have despaired and embarked for home, or have fallen victim to one of the many shrewd blows which the French continued to deliver almost to the last. At more or less

An imaginative romantic picture of the Pyrenees as they might have been when Wellington crossed them, by T. J. Barker, *c.* 1850.

cost to himself Wellington somehow contrived to turn every blow, and towards the end he had perfected a technique for delivering effective blows of his own.

Wellington himself admitted that on some occasions he would have been defeated if Napoleon had been present in the Peninsula. Not only did the Emperor's absence lead to a disgraceful lack of co-ordination between the French Marshals scattered around the various provinces, but it also deprived them of that peculiar genius for offensive warfare which might have carried them through the British line. The French commanders whom Wellington faced were often excellent strategists and 'grand tacticians'. They could manœuvre an army as well as he, and sometimes even better. But almost to a man they betrayed a certain lack of sustained impetuosity when they came close to the enemy. On many occasions they were outfaced by Wellington in circumstances where Napoleon would never have halted his forward march; while on other occasions their attacks lacked the flexibility and opportunism which Napoleon had sometimes displayed at the peak of his form. Victor at Talavera had come closest to achieving it, followed perhaps by Massena at Fuentes; but on other battlefields we have the impression that the Soults and the Marmonts abruptly ceased to function as soon as the guns began to shoot. They could take their war-horses to water, but they could not make them drink.

In 1815 in the Netherlands Wellington was finally confronted by Napoleon himself. There was a new energy about the French onset which must surely have made even the 'Iron Duke' wilt just a little, and all the more so since the allies were strategically wrong-footed from the start. At Quatre Bras the French fell upon a fraction of the Anglo-Dutch force and inflicted nearly 5,000 casualties, almost breaking the line. At Ligny the Prussians were 'damnably mauled' and forced to retreat with the loss of 20,000 men. Only on the field of Waterloo did Wellington gather his whole army, and he must have felt considerable apprehension when he contemplated the furious assault of which he knew Napoleon was more than capable.

In the event Wellington's army lost some 15,000 casualties at Waterloo, or about three times as many as in any of his battles up to that point. The Prussians lost a further 7,000 men in the same fight, which brought the combined allied total to almost 50,000 in the three days. However much we may fault the Emperor for his many tactical blunders ('Napoleon did not manœuvre at all', as Wellington exclaimed with more than a hint of professional disappointment)[17], we have to admit that the scale and ferocity of his attack was quite beyond anything in Wellington's previous experience. If this battle had been fought in the Peninsula there might well have been a decisive result to that contest, one way or the other, long before 1813. Indeed, it must have been the fear of just such a battle which had made Wellington so excessively cautious in 1810 and 1811.

The death of Picton at Waterloo. One of Wellington's most trusted tactical commanders, he never truly entered the Duke's inner counsels.

OVERLEAF: The casualties and carnage on the field of Waterloo, 'the morning after the battle'.

Waterloo was exceptional in Wellington's experience for another reason. It was the first time there had ever been a truly destructive pursuit at the end of one of his battles. In various ways this had been precluded even at Salamanca, Vitoria and Orthez. At Waterloo, however, the Prussians had eager cavalry at hand to take up the chase as soon as the battle itself had been won. They fell to their task with a will, and ensured that Napoleon could never rise again. This was certainly the most decisive of all Wellington's victories, and once again it is fascinating to speculate on what might have happened if he had ever managed to achieve a comparable result in the Peninsula.

There is no doubt that Wellington could have been beaten at either or both of Quatre Bras and Waterloo if only the French had played their cards a little better than they actually did. Nor is there much room for doubting that Wellington played his own cards remarkably well. Yet the very decision to stand and fight at Waterloo in order to make a junction with the Prussians on the battlefield was not at all a cautious one. So much might have gone wrong that Wellington would certainly have been forgiven if he had continued his retreat on 18th June and abandoned Brussels and Blücher to their

respective fates. Napoleon was finished anyway, since a vast avenging coalition was already marching against him from the ravaged plains of Eastern Europe. A victory at Waterloo was therefore by no means a precondition of final victory in the war. Wellington's assessment of the chances nevertheless turned out to be an accurate one and, although he was quite right in thinking it would be a near run thing, he was more than amply vindicated by the end result.

At Waterloo there was no opening for any of Wellington's 'Indian' offensives except at the level of minor tactics. At the higher levels he had to apply instead the lessons of some of his trickier defensive battles, notably Talavera and Fuentes. He did so in exemplary style, and probably never had a busier eight hours in all his life. He still found that things tended to go wrong whenever he was not present in person, so he took greater care than ever before to be present at the point of maximum danger. That he was not killed is a miracle, but that he succeeded in drawing the best from his men was in large measure a product of his calm energy and tireless attention to detail.

We have now come full circle and surveyed the whole of Wellington's eventful campaigning life. It was by no means either as untroubled or as free from blemishes as many writers would have us believe, nor was his art of war ever a fully formed or perfect entity. Wellington was forever revising his ideas in the light of new experiences, right up to what were for him the very novel circumstances at Waterloo. Even Waterloo was in a sense 'an experiment' for him, and there is some evidence to suggest that he may have been no less surprised than anyone else that he managed to carry it off so well. He rarely liked to reveal his inner thoughts, however, and like every good public figure he allowed an assumption to be made that he had been in full control of everything at all times. It may have been precisly this reticence, indeed, which first prompted his admirers to portray him in the now familiar terms as an iron and infallible commander. We might almost suggest that in a certain sense Wellington was instrumental in writing his own myth.

Behind the myth we may nevertheless occasionally catch a faint glimpse of a very different, more Tolstoyan figure. Certainly Wellington did impose his will on his army, and on military events, far more than Tolstoy might have thought possible.[18] On many occasions his manoeuvres were conducted with a full knowledge of causes and effects. Yet during certain periods of his career we have some reason to suppose that this admirable autonomy was attenuated by prescriptive systems of his own making. When he first came to the Peninsula he seemed to be trapped within the 'Indian' system of offensive warfare, and when this broke down at Talavera he resorted to an equally rigid 'cautious' system which in some ways restricted the enlightened exercise of his genius. Only in halting steps did he break free from these constraints to reach a higher understanding of the general's art. Even then, however, there always remained a possibility that circumstances might arise which he neither controlled nor fully understood. On a very few occasions Wellington seems to have recognised that he was being swept along on the flood tide of history, and that he could do no more than shut his eyes and launch out upon some dangerous course of action without any real confidence in the probable outcome. He seems to have taken a true gamble, in this spirit, both at Salamanca and at Waterloo. In both cases we sense a vulnerability and impotence which jars seriously with the myth, and we can only share his bemused relief when at the end of it all he discovers, to his astonishment, that the unfathomable maelstrom of events has stranded him finally upon a friendly shore.

CHAPTER 2

Wellington as an Attacking General – the Peninsular War

Too many historians, especially French historians who should know better, refer to Wellington as if he was primarily a defensive general. Even Field Marshals Wavell and Montgomery wrote, in identical words, 'Above all he was a master of defence.' A Scottish writer went so far as to write:

> Probably no general in history has ever had such an easy task as Wellington in the Peninsula. He had the game in his hands, and yet it took him nearly six years to advance from Lisbon to the Pyrenees.

This amounts to an accusation of defensive-mindedness, if not of actual timidity and so here I want to examine some of the reasons why the idea that he was primarily a defensive general has got about.

Let us look first at the whole Peninsular record as it is reflected in the actions fought under Wellington's own command which received battle honours. The first was Roliça, an attacking battle, and the second, Vimeiro, would have been fought on the offensive had it not been for Sir Harry Burrard's refusal to sanction any advance. As soon as he resumed the command Wellington launched a most dashing attack across the Douro at Oporto, an action I shall return to later. Talavera, later in the same year as Douro, finished being fought on the defensive because of the antics of Gregorio Cuesta, the Spanish commander. If Cuesta had not been, in Wellington's words, 'as obstinate as any gentleman at the head of an army need be',[1] the Talavera campaign would have been a headlong offensive aimed at Madrid since Wellington was hell-bent on striking straight at the heart of the French kingdom of Spain. 'The object,' he wrote, 'was to penetrate to Madrid at least.' In a semi-official letter, he was even more definite. 'The ball is at my feet, and I hope I shall have the strength to give it a good kick.'[2] In my opinion Cuesta, with all 'the whimsical perversity of his disposition', did Wellington a good turn by wrecking the joint plan. Had he not done so, the allied army would almost certainly have got to Madrid but,

Sir Henry Burrard, the doddering senior officer who dashed the fruits of victory from Wellington's hand at the end of the battle of Vimeiro.

for reasons Wellington could not expect or foresee, it would never have got back.

The next two battles, Busaco and Fuentes de Oñoro were certainly fought on the defensive but Fuentes was an example of the defensive-offensive since it was fought to cover the prosecution of an offensive act – the investment of Almeida. Next came the two great sieges Ciudad Rodrigo and Badajoz, certainly offensive actions and both, especially the second, undertaken with means that the sappers regarded as insufficient for the arcane mysteries of their craft. From then on, with one exception, all Wellington's Peninsular battles were fought on the offensive – Salamanca, a superb tactical offensive; Vitoria, the culmination of one of the greatest strategical offensives in all military history; Nivelle, which he believed to be his finest battle;[3] and then Nive, Orthez and Toulouse.

The exception was that great and underrated battle, Pyrenees. Here again it was a defensive-offensive battle because he was covering the sieges of two fortresses – San Sebastian and Pamplona – which were forty miles apart and separated by a substantial range of mountains. There were two other reasons why he had to be on the defensive in the Pyrenees. The first was that there was a truce on France's eastern front – the armistic of Pleischwitz – and, if past form was anything to go by, the eastern allies might well make peace and allow Bonaparte to turn his armies upon Wellington. The other reason was that the communications of Wellington's army had been extended by three hundred miles in little more than two months and, for the only time in the Peninsular war, the Royal Navy had fallen down on its job. Until supplies could arrive by sea Wellington was short of ammunition and almost everything else. The transports were at the mercy of French and American privateers unless they could sail in convoy and all the ships which should have provided the escorts were, in the words of the First Lord of the Admiralty, 'tearing themselves to pieces in long and distant voyages'[4] by which he meant that they had left their proper station in search of prize money.

To sum up the Peninsular record of battle honours – only five of the battles – Vimeiro, Talavera, Busaco, Fuentes and Pyrenees – were defensive and of these *two* were fought to cover sieges, one was the result of a mandatory order and one was the result of an aborted offensive. The fifth, Busaco, was fought when Wellington was retreating in the face of a greatly superior French army and it only happened because, when he found himself on one of the best defensive positions in Europe, he could not resist the temptation of letting Marshal Massena bash his head against a wall with minimal risk to the Anglo-Portuguese army.

I should not omit a reference to Wellington's most successful defensive action which did not get a battle honour because scarcely a shot was fired. This, of course, was Torres Vedras, an operation which lasted nearly a year and which cost the French army twenty five thousand men, more than any

A column of troops winds its way past one of the strong points of the lines of Torres Vedras.

battle they fought against Wellington with the possible exception of Waterloo – for which no reliable figures for the French loss have ever been produced.

Next I want to refer to two of the restrictions on Wellington's freedom of action when it came to deciding how his campaigns were to be waged. The first of these was the difficulty of obtaining replacements for losses sustained. While the army was inside the Lines of Torres Vedras, he remarked to Colonel Stanhope, 'I could lick those fellows any day, but it would cost me ten thousand men and, as this is the last army England has, we must take care of it.'[5] Eighteen months later in June 1812, when he was watching Marmont trailing his coat in the plain outside Salamanca, he said, almost to himself, 'Damned tempting! I have a great mind to attack them.'[6] Once again he restrained himself and for the same reason – he was commanding Britian's only field army and if he lost it, if it even became badly damaged, it could not be replaced.

It is easy to lose sight of how much of the army was committed to Wellington's command. At the beginning of 1813 the total strength of the British army was 255,000 rank and file and of these 65,000, more than a quarter, were directly under Wellington. Most of the remainder were in overseas garrisons from which they could not be withdrawn. There were 29,000 in the East Indies and 23,000 in the West Indies. 37,000 more were in the Mediterranean, in Gibraltar, Malta and Sicily, from where a strong detachment was operating on the east coast of Spain where it was partially under Wellington. There was a pitifully small army in Canada which was fighting off an American invasion which, fortunately, was abysmally mismanaged and there were odd detachments at the Cape, at Madeira, in New South Wales, at Goree in West Africa and on Heligoland. These garrisons, which had been pared to the bone since the turn of the century, absorbed about 110,000 men leaving about 80,000 to garrison the United Kingdom, including Ireland which needed something like an army of occupation. These 80,000 men included the depots of all the regiments serving overseas, consisting of raw recruits or men convalescent from service, and most of the Royal Veteran battalions whose members, even if they were not too old for active service, frequently were short of at least one limb.

Nor was there any hope of increasing the size of the army by recruiting. It was a good year in which the army could raise in the United Kingdom enough recruits to replace the annual wastage through disease, battle and desertion which ran at about 24,000 men a year. The only way in which the army could be kept up to strength was by taking on colonials and foreigners. In 1804 there had been 17,000 of them, eleven per cent of the total strength. By 1813 their number had risen to more than 53,000, one man in five. Some of these foreigners were very good indeed – like those of the better regiments of the King's German Legion – but some were the most dubious characters. Froberg's Albanians were, perhaps, an extreme case but most of the foreign recruiting had to be done from the prisoner of war camps and I for one would certainly not be happy to lead into battle a unit designated as the Regiment of German Deserters, even after it was retitled 8th battalion Sixtieth Foot. All the evidence is that when Wellington said that 'this is the only army England has', he was speaking the literal truth. If he suffered any serious loss the whole Peninsular campaign would have to be abandoned.

The second controlling factor was the effective size of the Peninsular army. As I have already said there were 65,000 rank and file on the books at the beginning of 1813 and of these 58,784 belonged to the army proper. The rest were gunners, sappers and commissariat personnel who came under either the Ordnance Office or the Treasury. Since they rendered separate returns it will only complicate matters if I start including them in the statistics so I am going to concentrate on the army which was subject to the Commander in Chief – the cavalry, the Guards and the infantry. Of the 58,784 men on the books on 1st January 1813, 17,698 were sick – three men in every ten. Admittedly January 1813 was a bad month for sickness, though it was by no means the worst, but after 1810 there was always a very high rate of sickness in the Peninsula. Even in a good month, such as June 1813, the rate was still sixteen per cent. After 1810 the rate swung between one

Battle casualties could expect only the roughest standards of treatment and a long absence from the ranks. These are some of the wounded at Waterloo.

man in six and one in three. By contrast the rate in the French army in Spain was relatively steady between one in eight and one in six. Thus the British sick rate at its best was the same as the French at its worst.

It is undeniable that the French in Spain suffered greater hardships than the British and there was little to choose between the efficiency of their medical services so we must look elsewhere to find the reason for the disparity between the sick rates. The reason can be stated in one word – Walcheren. Little historical attention has been expended on this disastrous expedition but one fact does emerge. 40,000 men were put ashore on Walcheren island and there were 106 deaths due to battle. 3,960 men died of disease and three months after the island had been evacuated 11,500 men were still in hospital.

Most of the Walcheren battalions were later sent to the Peninsula and they took Walcheren fever – probably malaria – with them and never got rid of it. Before they arrived the sick rate in the army was normally one in eight, the same as the French. Once they came it never fell below one in six and, as we have seen, sometimes reached one in three. In November 1812 the Ninth Foot, a Walcheren battalion, had sixty-five per cent of its men sick and the King's Own had sixty-three per cent. Nor was this the whole story. The fever permanently weakened a battalion. Wellington realised at an early stage that if he marched a Walcheren battalion too hard it retired to hospital. He himself wrote that 'The French troops march better than ours'[3] and Judge Advocate Larpent said 'In marching, our men have no chance at all with the French. The latter beat them hollow.'[8] Larpent thought that this was because the British ate and drank too much and there may be some truth in that (though it does not explain the Light Brigade's feat of marching on the way to Talavera) but I suggest that Walcheren fever

The rigours of the march weighed more heavily upon the British than upon the French.

was the true reason for the slower marching of the British. As far as I can discover no French regiment which served in the Peninsula had previously served at Walcheren and there is a probability that many of the French soldiers, especially those from the south, would be immune from malaria which was endemic in their birthplaces. Certainly the treatment for malaria would have been better in the British army since the only effective drug, Spanish bark – quinine – was kept out of France by the blockade. Indeed its exclusion was one of Bonaparte's complaints against the British on grounds of humanity.

Having dwelt on some of Wellington's disadvantages, I must say something about his advantages. He had the almost total support of the populations of Spain and Portugal. From the latter he obtained an army of more than 20,000 men which, thanks to Marshal Beresford, became good enough to be put into the line with British troops. Its only drawback was its supply system, which Beresford never managed to make efficient, and there were times – notably in early 1811 – when the Portuguese troops had to be left behind because there was no food for them. The Spanish army was a much more doubtful asset. The men were brave enough but they were usually badly led, and it would be a mistake to speak of their supply system because there was no system. They were usually short of food and on occasions succeeded in running out of ammunition. There was a very large number of Spanish troops, but only a small number could be counted upon to be in the right place at the right time and in a condition to fight.

Wellington's greatest help came from the vast mass of the Spanish people. As he said himself,

> It is true that the French defeat in Spain may in part be attributed to the operations of the allied armies; but a great proportion of it must be ascribed to the enmity of the people of Spain.[9]

The guerrillas could, and often did, make life intolerable for the French. Vast numbers of troops had to be kept in garrisons; every foraging party had to be conducted as a sortie from a besieged fortress; communications between the various French commands became difficult and at times impossible; intelligence was supplied to the British and denied to the French. It is reasonably certain that more Frenchmen died at the hands of the guerrillas than were killed by all the allied armies. Nevertheless there was a limit to what the guerrillas could achieve. The French armies in Spain amounted at their peak to more than 350,000 men and for most of the war there were at least a quarter of a million. In normal times most of them acted as a gigantic army of occupation but, if a real crisis arose, parts of the country could be abandoned and a huge field force concentrated. The French command knew that, in the long run, they could subdue Spain only if they could beat the British army. If Wellington looked like making a significant breakthrough, they had the possibility of producing enough troops to stop him. This is what happened in 1812.

The key to the fortress of Ciudad Rodrigo, captured by Wellington in 1812.

Since the beginning of that year Wellington had had a long winning run. He had taken Rodrigo and Badajoz, he had routed Marmont at Salamanca and he had marched triumphantly into Madrid. In mid-September he started to besiege Burgos which would have given him command of the main road to the French frontier. For the French this was a major crisis and they had to stop being an army of occupation and become a field force. They gave up the whole of Andalusia and withdrew most of their troops from the Biscay provinces. This gave them two columns which together amounted to 112,000 men and they could have got more if Marshal Suchet had been a little more cooperative. Against this Wellington had, in two separate corps, only 78,000 men of whom nearly a third were Spaniards. In terms of quality the French had a superiority of two to one. This was enough to push the allies back into Portugal and, in the opinion of most of the French army, it would have been enough to win the Peninsular War once and for all, if Marshal Soult had not lost his nerve on 15th November when Wellington offered him battle at Salamanca.

I want now to examine in rather more detail two of Wellington's attacking battles. First let us look at that strangely neglected action, the forcing of the Douro on 12th May 1809.

The background was that after Moore's army had been evacuated from Corunna, Soult invaded Portugal from the north with 23,000 men. He was under the impression that the British had left the country and, until he approached Oporto, the only effective opposition came from bands of peasantry. There was some attempt at a defence of the city by Portuguese regulars but Soult took it on 29th March. By that time his corps was in a fairly disorganised state and for the next six weeks he devoted himself to resting his troops and pacifying the country behind him. Meanwhile he pushed detachments south of the Douro to give warning of any danger.

During this time the British were trying to make up their minds what to do next. After much heartsearching they gave way to naval pressure that the bulk of the army's effort should be used to destroy the French naval base at Antwerp. That led to the abortive Walcheren expedition. Canning, as Foreign Secretary, insisted that troops should be sent to Cadiz to support the Spaniards. They were eventually sent only to find that the Spaniards did not want them and would not even let them land. Whatever was left over was sent to Portugal which, like Walcheren, was primarily a move designed to please the navy. Wellington was re-appointed to the command in Portugal with a small and distinctly 'second-eleven' type of army. The basis of it was the regiments which Moore had not thought good enough to take on his invasion of Spain. With a few exceptions the rest of the army was made up of under-trained second battalions because, with all the best trained battalions going to Walcheren, there were no other troops to send. Cavalry was in very short supply and there was not enough artillery, most of the guns which were with his army being only 3-pounders. With this rather miscellaneous collection, Wellington had not only to drive Soult out of northern Portugal but to keep an eye on another, larger French corps on the eastern frontier. All the British troops that could be spared for the Oporto operation were 16,000 British and so, to make up the numbers, he took with him 2,000 Portuguese. This was before Beresford had had a chance to work on them and when Wellington saw them he remarked, 'The men are very bad; the officers worse than anything I have ever seen.'[10]

Wellington had commanded in five major battles up to that time – Assaye and Argaum in India, Köge in Denmark, Roliça and Vimeiro in Portugal. In the first four he had always attacked. It was not his fault that he had had to defend at Vimeiro. Nevertheless Vimeiro and the subsequent Convention of Cintra had nearly brought his military career to an abrupt close and, at the Court of Inquiry, he had repeatedly been accused of rashness. It would not have been surprising if he had become a little cautious when he returned to the command. Far from it. He landed at Lisbon on 22nd April and within three weeks he was driving in Soult's posts. By the night of 11–12th May the army was on the Douro and, from the heights, could see Oporto below it on the north bank.

The problem was how to get across. The river was as wide as the Thames at Westminster and there was no bridge. The French had collected all the boats from the south bank. To make things more difficult there was no information about the strength of Soult's army, which seemed likely to be about as large as Wellington's own and was certainly more experienced. One might have expected Wellington to have taken time to consider the problem but he was all for attacking as soon as possible. He set his intelligence officers to finding some boats and sent for his heaviest guns – three companies of light six pounders – to form a battery on the heights over the river. By dawn all that could be found was a scuttled ferry boat four miles upstream

Marshal Soult, a former drill sergeant in the *Armée du Rhin* who intrigued to become King of Portugal, but who was roundly defeated at Oporto, 1809.

which was being hastily baled out and patched while nearer the town there was a skiff which a barber had hidden. With this Captain John Waters, one of Beresford's British officers, slipped across and, with some Portuguese help, brought back four wine barges, each capable of carrying thirty men. When Wellington heard of this windfall he remarked, almost casually – 'Well, let the men cross.'

Upstream at the ferry two battalions of the German Legion crossed with three squadrons of light dragoons. Their orders were to cut off the French retreat. The main attack went in on the four wine barges, a lift of only a hundred and twenty men. They crossed within a quarter of a mile of the eastern outskirts of Opporto but shielded from view by a projection of the southern heights. The Buffs went over first and it took six lifts, each lasting at least half an hour for the round trip, to get even that one battalion across: but in all that time the French were never alerted. As soon as each lift was across the men were stationed behind the walls of an unfinished convent and they were well established before the enemy noticed they were there. From then on there was really no contest. The French made several attacks

An excessively crowded depiction of the Oporto battle, which nevertheless gives a good idea of the steep cliffs on either bank of the Douro.

but against the Buffs (later reinforced by the 66th and 48th) firing from behind solid cover, they never stood a chance – particularly as they had eighteen guns firing at their outer flank at a range of less than five hundred yards. Each time Soult renewed his attack, he had to take troops away from the main city waterfront and, as soon as he had almost denuded it the citizens got into their boats, rowed across the Douro and brought another British brigade across. Oporto was taken for the loss of only eighty eight wounded and killed.

The only blemish on an otherwise perfect operation was the failure of the flanking attack to block the French retreat. The only interference the French suffered was from the light dragoons who sustained thirty five casualties in making a gallant but hopeless charge. The failure was due to the timidity of Brigadier John Murray, a singularly dim officer who was court-martialled for another incompetence four years later. Murray's failure highlights another of the restraints on Wellington. As he wrote in the following year;

When I reflect upon the characters and attainments of some of the General Officers of this army, and consider that these are the persons on whom I am to rely to lead

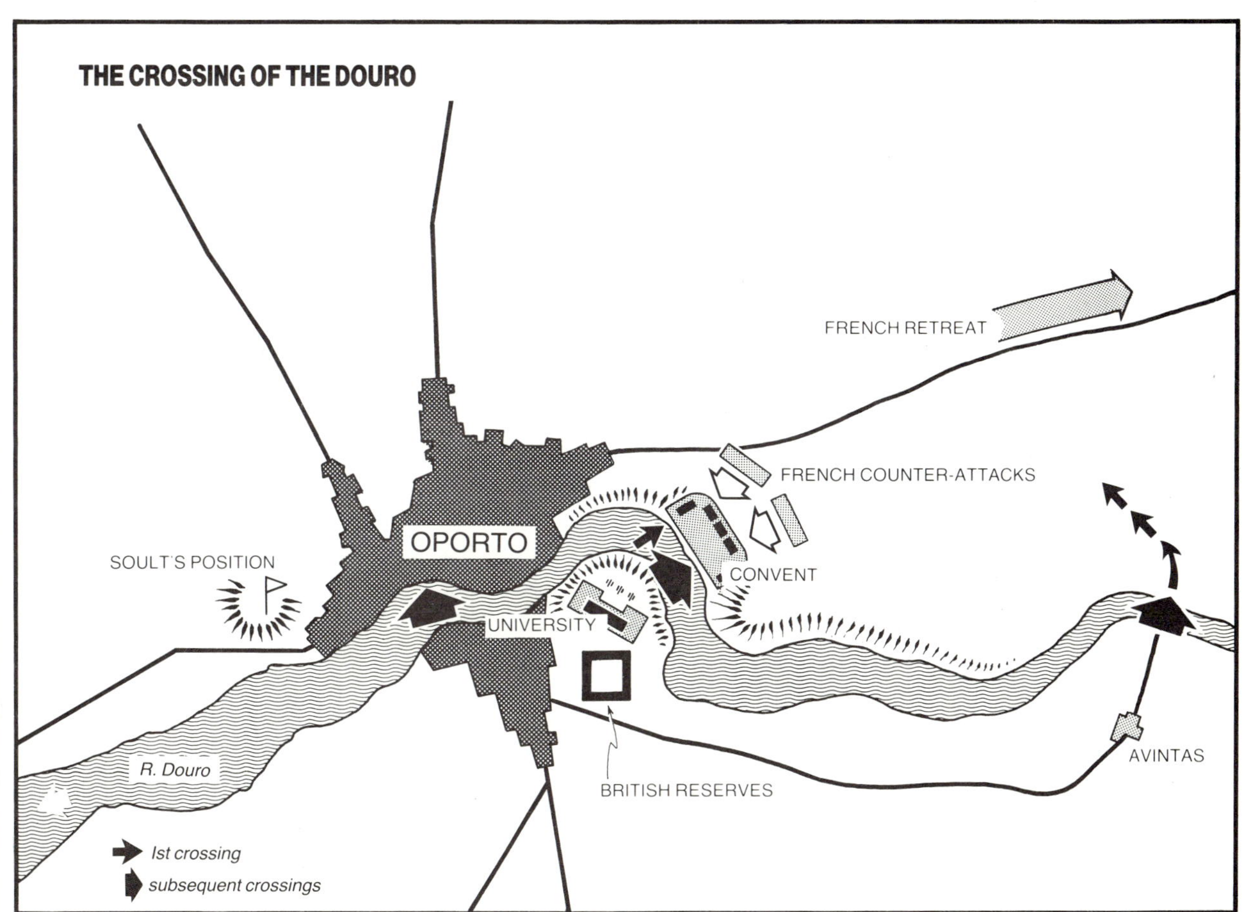

The bridge at Miserere, a choke-point on Soult's line of retreat from Oporto which had to be secured at the point of the bayonet before the remnants of the French army could pass.

columns against the French generals, and who are to carry my instructions into execution, I tremble; and, as Lord Chesterfield said of the generals of his day, 'I only hope that when the enemy reads the list of their names, he trembles as I do.[11]

I should add that it was not until 1813 that Wellington was given the right to send home unsatisfactory generals. Up to that time they were issued to him from London and he had to do the best he could with them. One, whom Sir John Moore had succeeded in having recalled, was sent back to serve in Portugal and the only thing Wellington could do with him was to keep him in Lisbon as permanent president of courts-martial. Then there was William Stewart who, he said, 'with the utmost zeal and good intention, cannot obey an order.'[12] Sir John Sherbrooke who, 'Is the most violent tempered person I ever met with, and there are no bounds to his folly when he is in a passion.'[13] There was Sir Brent Spencer who was 'exceedingly puzzle-headed. He would always talk of the Thames for the Tagus.' Above all there was Sir William Erskine 'upon whose sanity, I am sorry to say, much reliance cannot be placed.' When first told of his appointment, Wellington wrote to the Military Secretary in London, 'I have always understood him to be a madman.'[15] Quite unperturbed the Military Secretary wrote back, 'No doubt he is a little mad at times but in his lucid intervals he is an uncommonly clever fellow, though I must say he looked a little mad as he embarked.'[16] The truth of the matter is that Erskine had twice been confined as a lunatic, a fact that had not interfered with his career either as a soldier or as a member of Parliament. Incidentally he has the additional distinction of having the longest *errata* entry in the Dictionary of National Biography.

We must, however, get back to the forcing of the Douro and admit that Wellington's astonishing success owed much to the follies and neglect of Marshal Soult. The French commander had 13,000 men in and around Oporto which should have been more than enough to defend a substantial riverline on a narrow front in broad daylight. Unfortunately he made up his mind that his position in the city was unassailable and that Wellington would attack from the sea. He made his dispositions accordingly but on top of that he was culpably negligent in guarding the river bank and was asleep until after the Buffs were firmly established on the north bank. Soult was, however, one of the first generals in Europe and Wellington was in no position to assume that he would make every mistake open to him. It is arguable that Wellington was foolhardy, but it is quite impossible to maintain that he was thinking defensively.

Nevertheless, it was not until three years later that Wellington began to get a reputation as an attacking commander. After Salamanca the French general Foy wrote,

> Hitherto we had been aware of his prudence, his eye for choosing a position, and his skill in utilizing it ... At Salamanca he showed himself a great and able master of manoeuvre ... It raises him almost to the level of Marlborough.[17]

One might have expected that Foy would have appreciated Wellington's mastery of offensive manoeuvre rather sooner since he had been in command of the counter-attacks at Oporto. I do not, however, intend to deal here with Salamanca and will, instead, say something about Vitoria.

Vitoria is significant not so much for the battle itself but for the way in which the allied army got to the battlefield. This shows Wellington as a master of strategy. It was a strategic concept which compares well with the campaigns of Marengo and Jena, but with the advantage that Wellington found himself fighting the right battle at the end rather than, as Bonaparte did on both those occasions, fighting the wrong one.

To fill in the background, the Anglo-Portuguese army had been pushed back to Portugal at the end of 1812 with, as I have already mentioned, an appalling sick list. By the spring of 1813 things were much better and the field force available was 81,000 all ranks of whom there were roughly two British to one Portuguese. In addition there were initially 25,000 Spaniards available except that, just as the campaign got under way, they wrote a letter saying that they had no ammunition. Wellington's aim was to drive the French out of Spain. As he wrote in a private letter to the Secretary of State,

> I cannot have a better opportunity for trying the fate of a battle which, if the enemy should be unsuccessful, must oblige him to withdraw altogether.[18]

What this meant was that he intended to advance more than three hundred miles into an area in which there were not less than 125,000 effective rank and file of the French army who had the possibility of being substantially reinforced from the 50,000 men in Suchet's army on the east coast. On Bonaparte's orders the bulk of the French infantry – all but 33,000 of them – were to the north of the Ebro trying to put down the guerrillas. This meant that if Wellington was to get to the Pyrenees he would have to drive the French back on their reinforcements. His army was bound to get weaker as it marched three hundred miles forward while, in theory at least, the French would get stronger as they fell back on to their reserves. The thing could be managed only if the French could be hustled so fast that they would not have time to concentrate. If they managed to do so the allied army was likely to get defeated in a position from which it would be almost impossible to retreat.

The advance started in the last week of May. Wellington succeeded in convincing the French that he was going to attack up the Ciudad Rodrigo – Salamanaca road – the way he had advanced in the previous year – and the French decided that they would block him, again as they had done in 1812, on the line of the Douro north of Salamanca. Wellington duly did advance up the Salamanca road but he took with him only a small body of infantry covered by a large force of cavalry. The bulk of the Anglo-Portuguese infantry had already moved through northern Portugal by a mountainous route which the French had decided was impassable and, as soon as the French started to line the Douro, 50,000 men suddenly appeared behind their right flank, making their position untenable.

From then on it was only a matter of marching. Every time the French took up a position to make a stand, Wellington marched round their right flank. The only fighting was a few skirmishes in which the allies suffered

ABOVE: An artist's view of the Vitoria battlefield – a flat basin surrounded by mountains. Note that Wellington is personally confirming the topographical features with a local peasant.

TOP RIGHT: The open valley of Vitoria offered the French no strong defensive terrain, and their positions were quickly carried.

CENTRE RIGHT: Little Joseph Bonaparte, usurper to the Spanish throne and universally unsuccessful commander of armies.

BOTTOM RIGHT: Marshal Jourdan, King Joseph's senior military advisor on several occasions during the Peninsular War. A firey and energetic soldier in the 1790s, he appears to have lost his sureness of touch under the Empire.

only 200 casualties and on 20th June the main French armies were encamped around the city of Vitoria, having picked up only three of the eight divisions that were behind them. Although they were now only sixty miles from the French frontier, they had succeeded in losing five divisions which were milling round trying to find them. By that time the French command, led by King Joseph and Marshal Jourdan, had got so used to Wellington turning their right that they assumed he would do it again. On 21st June he changed his tactics and attacked them where they stood. He went for them in four columns working on exterior lines, an ambitious scheme which, because of the difficulties of timing, did not quite come off. Most of the personnel of the French army managed to get away but they left all their baggage and all their guns behind and they reached Pamplona with one howitzer between them. There was nothing they could do but retreat into France. That was the end of the Bonaparte kingdom of Spain.

There have been some criticisms of Wellington's tactics when he reached Vitoria. It has been said that by attacking in four columns, with only the most tenuous communications between right and left, he made life difficult for himself. He saw the problem quite clearly beforehand but he took the risk because it was the only plan which gave a chance of trapping the whole French army and he foresaw that, even if he failed in that, he would still achieve his main aim of driving them out of Spain and, since the Pyrenees were an excellent defensive position, of keeping them out.

As for those critics who maintain that Wellington was not good at following up his victories, I would suggest that first they check on the evidence and second that they remember some words which he wrote soon after Vitoria,

> It is a very common error among those unacquainted with military affairs, to believe that there are no limits to military success.[19]

A LA BELLE
ALLIANCE

CHAPTER 3

Wellington as a Coalition General

JOHN TERRAINE

Although I have been a great admirer of the Duke from boyhood, and this admiration has never faltered, I have never pretended to be any kind of expert in Wellingtonian studies. My approach to the subject of 'Wellington as a Coalition General', in fact, must necessarily be somewhat 'indirect'. Just *how* indirect will be clear when I explain that my starting point was in 1980, when I was turning over in my mind the qualifications chiefly of the British generals of the two World Wars of this century. This led me to attempt some sort of categorisation of generalship: its forms and functions; command-in-chief; command in battle; subordinate command; administration, organisation and so forth. This led me in turn to write an article along those lines for the British Army Review in April 1981, in which I said:

> It was Field Marshal Lord Slim who pointed out that the general has no other duty comparable to that of obtaining victory. Of course he was right. The winning (or loss) of victory must be the only possible starting point from which to make an assessment of a general. Whilst it is not the only consideration, I insist that it is the only *starting point*. Clearly, the next question is, 'What kind of victory?' The answer to that is naturally dependent on the kind of war. The toughest assignment in modern British military history (i.e. since the creation of our first real Regular Army, the New Model) has been command in war against the main body of a main continental enemy. Three British officers have undertaken such a task and brought it to a successful conclusion: the Duke of Marlborough, the Duke of Wellington and Field Marshal Lord Haig.

I remarked that Marlborough, between 1702 and 1713, was continuously engaged against the main armies and the best commanders of the most powerful nation on the European continent in his day – the France of Louis XIV; and I added:

> During that time he not only commanded the British forces engaged but bore the heavy responsibility of command-in-chief of the army of a coalition, which is a very different and much more difficult matter.

Marlborough's victorious career, I said,

Wellington and Blücher meeting at La Belle Alliance on the evening of Waterloo. In honour of the success of their coalition, Blücher suggested that the battle should be named after this roadside inn.

needs no comment beyond the remark that, as is usually the case, he had his bad days as well as his good –

and I propose to leave it at that.

Of Wellington I said that after a long apprenticeship fighting detachments of the main enemy,

Against the main body he was only engaged for a hundred days in 1815; on the other hand the enemy in question was Napoleon. One might reasonably say that quite a short time spent facing Napoleon could feel like a strenuous lifetime.

As regards Haig, I said that,

He cannot be described as a coalition C-in-C as Marlborough and Wellington had been. He was essentially a British commander whose army, though part of a coalition, found itself in three successive years engaging the main body of the main enemy, a unique circumstance in the British Army's history.

Haig's own 'Hundred Days' campaign in 1918, during which his armies took forty-nine per cent of all the prisoners taken by the coalition, and forty-three per cent of all the guns, ending with the Armistice, is also an unmistakable phenomenon, requiring no further comment.

It may be helpful to us, though, to think of some other examples of coalition generalship. It isn't easy until we come to the twentieth century; parallels for Marlborough and Wellington are hard to find. Indeed, it could be argued that Napoleon's long run of success was in large part due to his good fortune in never meeting – until 1815 – a real colaition general, or a coalition that really worked well on the battlefield; I would make no exception for Leipzig – the 'Battle of the Nations'. Nor does the rest of the nineteenth century offer any examples, though the World Wars of the twentieth naturally do.

In the First World War I would suggest that while Haig certainly showed the qualities required of a coalition general – as Sir John French did not – two Frenchmen went even further, showing the qualities of a coalition commander-in-chief. There were Joffre, who fulfilled the function from 1914 to 1916 without possessing the title, and Foch, in 1918, with the advantage of being officially 'Generalissimo'. One who conspicuously failed to show the qualities was Marshal Pétain, who was prepared to allow the coalition to fall to pieces in 1918. It was Haig's perception of this, and his immediate request that both Pétain and himself should be put under Foch (whom he knew to be a fighter) that saved the day and stamped him as a general in the true coalition mould.

In World War II the Western allies never met the main body of the main enemy after 1940. General Gamelin in that year showed himself to be more akin to Pétain than to Joffre or Foch – and Pétain himself was still Pétain. Later in the war, however, two Western commanders showed that they possessed in very great measure the qualities required to make a polyglot army work willingly and effectively together. They were General Eisenhower, in North Africa and North-West Europe, and Field Marshal Alexander in the Mediterranean. In the Far East Lord Mountbatten, at the head of South East Asia Command, was another who had the flair. The conspicuous failure in this connection was, of course, Field Marshal Montgomery, whose behaviour on more than one occasion in 1944 and 1945 threatened to damage the coalition severely.

In the post-1945 epoch, I think it is fair to single out General Matthew Ridgway as a man who could make an alliance work, and work within it; but it is clear that the talent is rare. In this matter – as in others – the Duke of Wellington belongs to a very restricted circle.

It is appropriate to ask at this stage what *are* the talents of a coalition commander? What qualities does he have to display? There are two, I think, which are pre-eminent. First, he must have absolute belief, and be seen to have absolute belief, in the coalition which he serves as a means of making war. He must understand, absolutely, the *need* for the coalition and the need to keep it in being. That was the difference between Pétain and Haig in 1918; that was what made Eisenhower rise above all the frustrations, all the unfulfilled agreements, all the infuriating behaviour – and in this connection let us remember that he had to deal not only with Field Marshal Montgomery, but also with such a varied array of perplexing personages as (on their own ground) General Giraud, Admiral Darlan, General de Gaulle, other buccaneers of the Free French movement, and the Communist-inspired Resistance. So obviously the patience of Job needs to be written into the job specification.

Secondly, the true coalition commander must be absolutely trusted. He must put the interests of the coalition above national interests, above personal interests – and he must be known to do this. In Eisenhower's words, the coalition commander must know that 'immediate and continuous loyalty to the concept of unity . . . is basic to victory.'[1] Like so many of the gravest matters in war, it all sounds elementary. But it is not elementary. On the contrary, it is against all instinct, and against all training, not to think first of one's nation, one's army and one's own career in it.

So now, back to Wellington. The first thing I learned, when I investigated this subject from his point of view, was something that I was certainly not aware of in 1980, when I wrote my article for the British Army Review. I had thought of him then in terms of the Peninsular War and the Waterloo campaign, but I now discovered that his true apprenticeship for coalition command had been in India. The phrase 'Sepoy General' has been applied to Wellington in a derogatory sense not only by Napoleon's propaganda-scribes on the *Moniteur* and elsewhere, but also on this side of the Channel, with the suggestion that commanding sepoys in Indian battles could have no bearing on European warfare.

It was nonsense. In fact, the opposite was true. As S. G. P. Ward said, in a perceptive little study in 1963, 'The vast experience he had gained in

India was the foundation of all his subsequent success.'[2] Not least in that experience was the conduct of coalition war.

We have to bring our imaginations to bear at this point, since after nearly four decades of Indian independence, following nine decades of the Raj, the India of 1800 is hard to picture. Indian unity, which was the great issue bedevilling independence in 1947, was a very remote concept when Wellington went out in 1796. The only unity that India had ever known – the Moghul Empire – was in its final dissolution. Indian society was fragmented, and the power structure was fragmented; the only place where power did *not* reside being with the Moghul Emperor in Delhi, who was virtually the prisoner of his own so-called vassals.

Right across central India sprawled the huge territory known as the Mahratta Confederacy – a confederacy only in name, because the five great princes, or warlords, of the Mahrattas were independent and often at war with each other. Their power was founded on large armies of light horsemen, who lived off the land. They were predators of evil reputation, and none worse than the mercenaries they recruited from all parts, known as Pindaris. These were feared and loathed wherever they went. Ridding the people of this scourge was one of the most important factors in making the rule of the British East India Company acceptable.

Around the fringes of the Mahratta lands were the states of the other great princes: the Nizam of Hyderabad (in theory the Emperor's viceroy in the South) and the Sultan of Mysore, further south still. These three –

Baggage of an army on the march in India. Although this picture was drawn a generation later than Wellington's Indian campaigns, the scene must have been unchanged from his day.

Mahrattas, Hyderabad, Mysore, formed the triad around which East India Company politics revolved in southern India. To the North there was the Kingdom of Oudh, the dominions of the Rajput princes and the growing power of the Sikhs in the Punjab. And everywhere you looked there were the smaller fry; the nawabs and rajahs, the débris of over 2,000 years of history, all with their own ambitions, their own policies to pursue. It is not difficult to imagine the permutations, the changing patterns of treaties and alliances within this kaleidoscope.

British power in India, at the turn of the eighteenth and nineteenth centuries, was not to be compared with what it became in the next fifty years. Except for the great province of Bengal, conquered by Clive, British power, too, was fragmented and frail by comparison with the great forces that surrounded it. Only by making treaties and alliances with those forces could it hope to survive and expand. And, of course, one of the chief practitioners of British expansion was Richard Wellesley, Lord Mornington, the Duke's elder brother, who became Governor General in 1798.

From then until Richard Wellesley's departure it was all action in India, and this was when Arthur Wellesley felt for the first time the stimulating tug of the reins of power in his own hands. This was, in effect, his military academy. It is, to my mind, absolutely characteristic that, in playing the large part that he did in executing his brother's policies (and also, it may be added, in offering his brother much advice on which the policies might be found or by which they might be modified) Arthur Wellesley kept a clear

LEFT: A crude print of the storming of Seringapatam. Compare this with –

BELOW: A more highly finished version of the same. Note that the cannon in the foreground has been accurately drawn from life, even though much of the rest springs only from the artist's imagination.

object in mind. 'The hypothesis upon which all Indian politics should turn' – to use his own words – was the consideration whether a policy improved or weakened the British position in a war with France.

War with France: not simply war with some Indian prince or princes for local reasons; not war to improve the trading opportunities of the East India Company; certainly not war to acquire territory for its own sake: war with France, the 'theme music' of his entire military life.

French power in India, needless to say, was by now the merest faint shadow of what it had once been – but it was still there. French soldiers trained and commanded the armies of Indian princes; French adventurers carved out fiefs of their own under the overlordship of the most powerful maharajahs, like Sindhia the Mahratta; French traders brought in weapons. And always there was the fear of a descent – in alliance with one or more of the princes – of a French army, carried by a French fleet, from Mauritius.

Arthur Wellesley did not rate this risk high, but it exercised his brother. For Arthur,. the purposes of treaties and alliances was to rule it out, with military action a poor second. But if there *had* to be military action – and with a Governor-General of large ideas like Richard it was inevitable that there would be – then the treaties and alliances were essential for other reasons. They provided the *manpower* for the ensuing wars; they provided the *horsepower* which was essential for campaigning against mobile enemies like the Mahrattas and Pindaris; they provided the *stores and magazines* without which the armies could not operate; and they provided the *bullock-power* without which the armies could not move. 'Bullocks,' says Philip Mason (referring to the Mahratta War) 'are the subject of half his letters and no word recurs more frequently'.[3] And so, from the first, Wellesley understood in India that *his allies were the sanction of all his actions.* There he learned the disciplines of coalition war – and generally speaking they are hard ones.

One of the Seringapatam guns used in the print of the storming, below. This fine piece is part of a pair which today adorns the Officers' Mess at the Royal Military Academy, Sandhurst.

In his first campaigns, against Mysore and certain freebooters who infested the country after the fall of Seringapatam, he had 'more or less friendly' Mahratta allies, and learned what was involved in trying to cooperate with them. In the war against the Mahrattas, 1802–03, he was in alliance with the Nizam of Hyderabad; by now, says Richard Aldington, 'he had a complete understanding of the nature of allies'.[4]

He needed it; he needed that patience of Job of which I wrote earlier; and whether negotiating with enemies or friends he had to meet, in Aldington's words, 'the interminable crafty or childish excuses for delay and more delay with smiling patience.'[5] This, of course, has always been a great test for Europeans operating in the East in peace or war. It puts one in mind of a story of a lecture which was once given on the subject of the Irish Gaelic tongue. At the end of the talk the lecturer was asked whether there is any Gaelic word expressing the same meaning as the Spanish '*mañana*'. 'It is interesting that you should ask that,' he replied. 'We do in fact have about

a dozen words approximating to the meaning of *mañana*, but none conveying quite the same degree of urgency.' After India, *mañana* must have sounded urgent indeed; and quite soon the Duke would be learning all the meanings of *mañana*.

PREVIOUS PAGES: The sons of Tipoo Sahib being handed over as hostages – one of many techniques open to the British in India for the cementing of alliances.

There was, perhaps, one other lesson about alliances that he may have brought back from India: the need to have at one's disposal a hard core of entirely reliable troops of one's own when time runs out, when swift and decisive action is essential, and there is no more time for talk. Such an occasion was his great Indian victory at Assaye, on 23rd September 1803, when he completely defeated the Mahratta army of 50,000 men and more than 100 guns, with only his own Anglo-Indian army of 5,000 with 17 guns. It was this battle that made the 'Sepoy General' a famous general. The lessons he learnt in it, and in all his Indian experience, enabled him, when the next test came, to make a famous army.

The next test was the Peninsula – not the brief, successful foray of 1808, whose results were thrown away by the old Horse Guards generals, but the Peninsula in 1809, when he was really in command. And by virtue of being really in command, the management of the new coalition with Portugal and Spain was effectively in his hands.

'Coalition with Portugal and Spain'. Let us look at that phrase a little more closely. As Mr Ward says, the Peninsular War means different things to different people. Each member of the coalition had his own view-point:

> To the Spaniards it is the struggle of a whole nation rising against a tyrannical foreign government, a movement in which our army plays but a marginal part. To the Portuguese it means principally the frustration of three cruel invasions: in this our share is fully acknowledged, but the climax of the war lies beyond the boundaries of national concern ... the Peninsula claims *our* interest as the one theatre in which the military effort of this country ... was successfully exerted to contribute to Napoleon's downfall ...[6]

The pattern in the Peninsular War can thus be seen as an alternation of interests coinciding, drifting apart, coming together again, or not, as the case may be.

Portugal was the first ally, and well illustrates one of the fundamental maxims of coalition war: that the strength of a coalition is, in effect, the strength of the strongest ally or, to put it another way, the strongest ally will always call the tune. Portugal in 1809 was very far from strong. She had already endured two invasions in eight years: invasion by the Spanish in 1801 and by the French in 1808, at first with Spanish support. There was no reason for the Portuguese to love the Spanish, even though for the time being their interests did coincide. The British, however, having demolished the French invasion of 1808, were very popular in 1809, and Wellington's position was very strong.

In a flush of enthusiasm the Portuguese Regency made him Marshal-General of their forces. This might, of course, have been just an honorary

Wellington as Portuguese Marshal-General, *c.* 1814, with maps of his Portuguese victories spread before him.

Beresford in his uniform as Marshal commanding the Portuguese army.

designation – a pleasant gesture. There was, after all, already an English officer in Portugal with the rank of Marshal and the title of Commander-in-Chief – General Beresford, a gigantic Irishman with a flair for organisation, who had the daunting task of reorganising the decrepit Portuguese Army, training it, and turning it into a useful fighting force.

Wellington had other things to do. He wanted two things from Portugal: a secure base for operations against the French in the Peninsula, and an effective army to back up his British contingent which, he knew, would never be all that strong in numbers. What the Portuguese wanted from Britian was, above all, to see the French kicked out. But it was no good kicking them out if they came back again – which they did, in 1810; so the Portuguese were prepared to support Wellington loyally until the French threat had been evidently removed – and as long as British money lasted to pay for their military needs.

The money did last; and in 1809 the French threat was still strong enough for Wellington to insist that, in Napier's words, 'his authority as marshal-general of Portugal should be independent of the local government, and absolute over all arrangements concerning the forces'. It meant that when Beresford had made him a Portuguese army, he would be able to give it direct orders, and use it precisely as he saw fit – an unusual state of affairs in coalitions, certainly a very far cry from Marshal Foch's delicate position as Allied Generalissimo in 1918, and far enough from Wellington's own position *vis-à-vis* the Spanish.

It took Beresford about a year to get his Portuguese army ready. At Busaco in September 1810 Wellington had 51,000 men present, about half of them Portuguese. In January 1812, out of 56,000 men present in the ranks, 21,000 were Portuguese. At the siege of Badajoz in April that year, almost exactly half those present were Portuguese – just under 11,000. At Salamanca in July they numbered 17,500, out of just under 43,000. In July 1813, after Vitoria, they formed one third of his army – 22,000 out of 66,000 – and, most remarkable of all, at Toulouse, the final battle in April 1814, there were still 21,000 Portuguese out of a total of 64,000. They were a long way from home; Beresford had worked well. But as the war moved away from Portugal enthusiasm for it waned, and so did the enthusiasm for the British alliance and the hard disciplines of coalition war.

It was after Vitoria, after the retreat from Moscow, with Napoleon in obvious difficulties in Germany and calling for reinforcement from the Peninsula – in other words, with victory in sight – that the sharpest Anglo-Portuguese crisis arose. Only three years after the expulsion of the French, in Napier's words, 'the nation was quite ready to shake off the burden of gratitude'. Above all, there were voices loudly demanding that they should shake off the military subservience – the British officers commanding Portuguese regiments, the brigading of Portuguese with British troops, the British Commander-in-Chief. They wanted their own army – a natural enough desire; but as Wellington told them, 'separated from the British, the Portuguese army could not keep the field in a good state although their government were to incur ten times the expense under the actual system'.

Above all, there was no Portuguese officer of stature to command it, and definitely none that they could agree on themselves. So the demand came to nothing – but the rancour remained. And inside Portugal, after all that had been achieved together, anti-British sentiments bubbled up and ran over, and the soldiers themselves – Portuguese as well as British – were ill treated by the people they had saved. Wellington was disgusted; he said: 'The British army which I have the honour to command has met with nothing but ingratitude ... I hope however that we have seen the last of Portugal!'[7] And so it proved, which was just as well, because 1814 would show, as 1918 and 1945 would also show, that nothing is more lethal to an alliance than victory, nothing more disastrous than success.

If that seems a sour note on which to end the story of the Portuguese alliance, it is positively rapturous by comparison with what we find when we look at Spain. Sir Charles Oman suggests, with some reason, that the Spanish war effort has had a 'bad press' from British writers (including Napier, and Wellington himself) because 'It chanced that our countrymen did not get a fair chance of observing their allies under favourable conditions.'[8] The old Spanish regular army, he says, 'had been practically destroyed before we came upon the field', and ill luck threw into Wellington's way some of the very worst of the Spanish generals. This is no doubt quite true, but I think there is something else as well that has to be taken into account – a special hazard attaching to the Anglo-Spanish alliance. It is not a common circumstance – and certainly not a helpful one – for two nations to pass directly from a state of war with each other into an alliance. Yet this is what happened in 1808, and not by the desire of either but through the arbitrary action of a third power hostile to both – Napoleon's annexation of Spain by the act of putting his brother on the Spanish throne.

Although badly disappointed by the antics of Spanish field armies, Wellington must have been delighted by the successes of guerillas such as the followers of this plausible but lethal officer – Francisco Espoz y Mina. Mina later served with distinction under Wellington's direct command, in the Pyrenees.

At the time that he did so, Britain and Spain were actually (though not very actively) at war; they had, in fact, been at war for eleven of the preceding thirteen years. The latest outbreak of war between them had been caused by the, no doubt prudent but unquestionably high-handed, seizure of the Spanish treasure fleet by the Royal Navy in October 1804. A year later came the destruction of the Spanish navy at Trafalgar, with ten out of fifteen ships lost. So the Spanish – a people not in any case well disposed towards foreigners at any time – had good reason to detest their new allies very heartily. And to tell the truth, this frame of mind was reciprocated.

Spain was Britain's true 'traditional enemy'. The conflict had deep roots and in those years of naval strife and invasion threats, memories of the

A gunner, an infantryman and a dragoon of the Spanish regular army.

Spanish Armada were vividly reawakened. Napoleon himself served to remind the British of Philip II, the Inquisition, the Duke of Parma's army hovering across the Channel – in other words, everything that they hated most. These were poor auspices for the experience which Aldington calls 'the horrors of cooperating or trying to cooperate with Spanish generals'. He goes on to speak of the 'delays, disappointments and discomfiture which awaited the commander who expected punctual and effective support' from the Junta which was the govering body of Spain in 1809. Evidently deep draughts would have to be drawn from the reserves of Job-like patience – and it was no bad thing to be a 'Sepoy General' with a good grounding in the theory and practice of *mañana*.

Perhaps it is as well, looking back with all the detachment that distance in time can offer, that Wellington's first practical experience of his Spanish allies was what it was. He entered Spain for the first time on June 27th 1809, at which stage, says Napier, 'Sir Arthur, never having seen the Spanish troops in action, thought too well of them; and having no experience of Spanish promises, trusted them too far.'[9]

He was soon disillusioned. What followed was the Talavera campaign; it was, as Oman says, 'the first in which English and Spanish troops stood side by side', and he agrees that 'there can be no doubt that the latter (with few exceptions) behaved in their very worst style'. And worst of all was their general, the Spanish Captain-General, Cuesta, who has become a by-word for abominable behaviour towards an ally. We can scarcely do better than attend to the words of Philip Guedalla on Cuesta:

This paladin, now rising seventy, was less menacing as an adversary than as an ally; for he looked back upon an uninterrupted record of sanguinary (and frequently avoidable) defeat. Composed in equal parts of pride and failing health, he was the embodiment of Spain at its very worst – old, proud, incompetent and ailing – and Sir Arthur could hardly hope to have a more instructive object-lesson in the joys of allied operations.'[10]

Wellington did his best to handle this objectionable old man, and succeeded in winning the Battle of Talavera in spite of him, but the whole experience left a mark that could not be effaced; a distrust of Spanish generals which lasted for the rest of the war.

This first campaign in Spain in 1809 left two more marks as well. First it gave Wellington the measure of the Spanish Army. On the evening before the battle he witnessed an extraordinary scene: some French light cavalry were pushing forward a reconnaissance in the direction of Talavera itself, where Cuesta's army was drawn up. They were still a long way away – well out of range – but the whole Spanish line suddenly delivered a tremendous volley and then, said Wellington,

Two thousand of them ran off ... not 100 yards from where I was standing, who were neither attacked, nor threatened with an attack, and who were only frightened by the noise of their own fire. They left their arms and accoutrements on the ground, their officers went with them, and they plundered the baggage of the British army, which had been sent to the rear. Many others went, whom I did not see.[11]

Napier says it was 10,000 men in all, taking with them all the artillery, part of which was still missing in the battle the next day. Needless to say, this episode made a considerable impression on the Duke. It showed him an army which was in almost as lamentable a state (though larger and better equipped) as the Portuguese – but without any possibility of the Portuguese remedy. There would be no Beresford for Spain – Spanish pride forbade it; and Spanish pride forbade also the attachment of British officers to Spanish regiments for training purposes. Spanish pride, and I dare say an admixture of the mutal national dislike which I referred to earlier, also ruled out raising any significant number of Spanish troops in the British service. Such is the significant difference between relations with a small ally and relations with a large one.

Secondly, there was the matter of Spanish promises. When he entered Spain, the Junta assured Wellington that 'every needful article should be forthcoming' to supply the British army. Accordingly, he entered his allies' country virtually without supplies, and almost without transport, relying on this assurance. He would never do that again; the supplies were not provided, and as Napier says

No means of transport had been provided for him, his troops were on half allowance, absolute famine approached, and when he demanded food he was answered with false excuses and false statements.[12]

It was so bad that he even threatened to withdraw from Spain altogether – and that was, in fact, what he had to do not long afterwards. It was a lesson he never forgot. Thereafter, as Aldington says, he was

> grimly determined never again to trust the promises of a Spanish Junta, never again to cooperate with a Spanish army unless he could command it.

Later in the war, after the battle of Salamanca, and in the euphoria of the first French retreat from Madrid, Wellington received the title of Captain-General of the Spanish Army. It was only a title; it never conferred on him anything even remotely resembling the powers he had received from the Portuguese, but it did give him a measure of command over the Spanish contingents that fought alongside him, with varying levels of performance, in the latter stages of the war. The relationship was never happy.

Such, then, was the alliance with Spain. The miracle was that it survived as it did for over six years. That it did so was largely due, it must be said, to the French, whose fighting capacity on the one hand, and shocking behaviour on the other, helped greatly in keeping their enemies united despite themselves. Oman, who found the Duke's autocratic manner and sarcastic style of speech distasteful, blames him for what he calls 'his unveiled scorn, and his outspoken exposure of all their meanesses', and suggests that 'A little more diplomatic language would have secured less fric-

A major resource which Wellington expected from his Spanish allies consisted of billeting for his army. Unlike that of the French, the allied system of finding and paying for billets was regularly organised.

tion, and probably better service.'[14] Frankly, I doubt it; both countries were at a low ebb, irrespective of the war and Wellington. Portugal, once one of Europe's most active sea-faring nations, and Spain, once her pre-eminent military power, were both deeply sunk in sloth, corruption and incompetence, far beyond the power of smooth talk to mend. Indeed, it could be argued that smooth talk would have made matters worse, and an abrasive tongue like Wellington's was badly needed.

I am certainly convinced that, having acknowledged the prime rôle of the French in cementing this unlikely alliance, we must give all remaining credit to the infinite patience, far-sighted sagacity and iron nerve of the 'Sepoy General'. Beating the French in the field never presented half of the difficulties of dealing with his perplexing, exasperating, but always essential allies.

That might be our last word on the Peninsular War, but for one highly significant consideration. By 1813 it was not just a matter of the coalition within the Peninsula itself; the campaign had to be related to that of the much larger coalition which was beating Napoleon to his knees in Germany – a coalition which comprised the empires of Russia and Austria, the kingdoms of Prussia and Sweden, and an Anglo-German (chiefly German) contingent. To this large, but unwieldly and somewhat uncertain array of allies,

LEFT: William Prince of Orange, wounded at the moment of victory at Waterloo. This young prince was an ally of great value to Wellington at the strategic level, but something of a liability when it came to his tactical decisions.

RIGHT: Frederick William III of Prussia – one of Britain's staunchest allies in the crucial years 1813–15.

Wellington contributed two things: first, great encouragement, after his climactic victory at Vitoria in June, and his advance to the French frontier. Secondly, the tying down of large forces of trained, hardened French troops. As late as September these still numbered 170,000 – the half of whom at Leipzig in October could have given history a very different twist.

And so we come to 1815 and Waterloo, the final act of the Duke's military career. Because attention, for so many obvious reasons, tends to concentrate on the Battle of Waterloo and the brief campaign of which it was the climax, it is often forgotten that 1815 was once again a year of coalition war on the grand scale, with six allied armies in the field:

> The Duke's own Army of the Netherlands
> Blücher's Prussian Army of the Lower Rhine
> Prince Schwartzenburg's Austrian Army of the Rhine
> A large Russian army assembling behind the Rhine
> A Bavarian army, also on the Rhine
> and an Austro-Italian army, threatening southern France.

Furthermore, the Duke's army itself was very much a coalition army, with the British contingent (i.e. the contingent present on the battlefield on 18th June) numbering only some 24,000 out of 68,000. The others were the King's German Legion (which counted as part of the British Army, but was British only in the administrative sense) – almost 6,000 strong; nearly 18,000 Dutch-Belgians; 11,000 Hanoverians; nearly 6,000 Brunswickers, and a Nassau contingent of nearly 3,000. This last serves to illustrate the peculiar hazards of commanding such armies. At one point during the battle, the Duke was about to ride across the face of a square of Nassau troops. Some of his staff reminded him that only a year earlier these men had been serving Napoleon, and they were still wearing the uniform of their French service. They persuaded him to pass at the rear of the square, rather than the front; which was possibly just as well, because as one of the battle's contemporary narrators says, 'the simple process of pulling a single trigger might have blasted all our expectations.'[15]

I will not dwell on the familiar story of Waterloo except to make two points. First, it was in all respects a coalition victory. It was fought on the strength of a clear agreement between Wellington and Blücher, an agreement which Blücher faithfully kept, as Wellington was confident that he would. Disputation about whether the victory really belonged to one or the other is beside the point.

Secondly, I would remark that commanding a coalition army within the framework of an even larger coalition, though outwardly a massive and daunting task, was in fact far less so than the business of commanding in the Peninsula, because Wellington came to it in 1815 with all the prestige of his Pensular victories behind him.

He was no longer a 'Sepoy General', he was Europe's premier soldier – and that does make a difference!

PART TWO

Wellington and Waterloo

CHAPTER 4

Waterloo: Wellington's Eye for the Ground

DAVID HOWARTH

Among my pet dislikes are historians who say that generals of the past made blunders, and imply that if they'd been there themselves they would have made a better job of it. It's my belief the Duke made not a single blunder, no avoidable mistake at all, in the Waterloo campaign. He acted on his own wide experience and the information he possessed. Some of that information was erroneous, but that was no fault of his. And one can admire a man's skill without suggesting it was supernatural.

Yet the story has grown up that by some magical foresight he had used his eye for the ground to inspect and approve the battlefield of Waterloo some weeks in advance. On the contrary, *all* the circumstantial evidence is against it. I am certain that Wellington's dispositions at Waterloo were made partly by improvisation and partly in response to Napoleon's movements.

To begin with, there are and were at least six main roads from the French frontier up to the neighbourhood of Brussels, and Wellington could not know which of them Napoleon would advance by. And to choose a field of battle would surely have been a waste of time when the chances were five to one Napoleon would come another way. Indeed when the Duke was told just before the Duchess of Richmond's ball that the French had crossed the frontier at Charleroi, he went on believing the main force would come from farther west, somewhere in the direction of Mons or Lille. He sent his own main strength in that direction, and was only able to bring it quickly back because of the transverse road that crossed at Quatre Bras. And all through the battle of Waterloo, he kept a force far out on that western flank at Hal. This was one of the moments when his information was wrong. Either his own rather unreliable spies in France had let him down, or else the much more numerous and efficient French spy system in Belgium had planted the erroneous idea on him. Belgium was full of Bonapartists.

Dramatic news from Ligny ruffles the feathers at the Duchess of Richmond's ball. Ladies may swoon, but Wellington is inspired to heroic measures!

We do know, of course, that he rode down the Charleroi road, through Waterloo, Mont St Jean and the village of Genappe, on the morning of 16th June when the ball was over. I'm no horseman, but that ride always seems to me to have been a surprising feat – right down to Quatre Bras, across to Ligny where Marshal Blücher had chosen to make his stand, back to Quatre Bras and up to Waterloo again; at least fifty miles on rough stony roads, and on the same horse, Copenhagen, that he rode through the whole campaign.

I suggest it was then, two days before the battle, that he first saw that valley at Waterloo, or more correctly Mont St Jean. By then, he would have looked at it with more immediate interest. He knew then that Napoleon's right wing was facing the Prussians at Ligny, and that another force under Marshal Ney was facing him at Quatre Bras. There might still have been a third force somewhere to the west, but the choice of roads had narrowed. He knew that if Marshal Blücher was forced to retreat from Ligny, he would have to retreat in parallel from Quatre Bras, up the road he was riding down. So a defensive position on that road had become of paramount importance.

Copenhagen, Wellington's trusted and highly intelligent charger (1808–36). He is buried at Stratfield Saye, Wellington's country seat in Hampshire.

But there's one other thing I would like to point out about that road. The valley at Mont St Jean was the only place on it he could conceivably defend. *I* don't claim to have an eye for the ground in any military sense, but I have driven up and down that road a good many times, and I don't think he needed *his* undoubted eye for the ground to choose that valley. It's just possible a battle might have been staged across the valley at Genappe, with the stream and the village in the bottom: that was a position not entirely unlike Ligny. But if he had to retreat from Quatre Bras, Genappe was not far enough. He would still have been out on a salient, in danger of being surrounded. From Genappe to the Inn of La Belle Alliance, on the edge of the other valley, the countryside was a maze of little hills with no decisive valley among them; no distant views, only small fields with hedges and copses. It still is, and I think it was probably more heavily wooded then than it is now. In a populous country like Belgium, trees always tend to be cut down and cleared, not planted. That has certainly happened round Quatre Bras.

TOP: The main road to Brussels where it passes La Haye Sainte farm and ascends the northern side of 'the valley' towards the centre of the allied position.

BOTTOM: La Belle Alliance – a landmark in the centre of the French lines, but still some way forward from Napoleon's headquarters.

Then north of that valley, north of Mont St Jean and the village of Waterloo, it was practically solid forest all the way to Brussels. It still is, because that's a state forest and strictly preserved. One might imagine now that a forest would be a perfect place to stop an advancing army, with the short-range weapons they had at that time. Anywhere on those last ten miles or so of the road, defenders might have ambushed advancing troops, disorganised them with musketry and decimated them with grape, and then vanished among the trees to re-load. But evidently, nobody then was thinking in terms of ambush. That was not their idea of a battle. What they were looking for was a wide open space, where infantry could form a line that was visible from one end to the other, and carry out their parade-ground movements in formation; and above all where cavalry could perform unimpeded the charges they felt were the proper way for a gentleman to fight. Those, not ambush, were the accepted battle tactics.

Now, my point so far is this: although the Duke had an eye for the ground which never failed, he hadn't used it or needed it in choosing the field of battle at Waterloo. As soon as he knew that was the road that Napoleon threatened him on, he had no choice. On the 16th when he rode down the whole of that road, he couldn't have failed to see that that valley was the one and only place for the sort of set battle he expected.

There's one other small bit of evidence that suggests this was the first time he had seen it. That is the business of the maps. We are told that on the day of battle the whole army had two copies of a sketch map of the field between them. The Prince of Orange had one, and Sir William de Lancey had the other in his pocket. Now marine cartography had made enormous progress in the eighteenth century, with the inventions of the sextant and chronometer. But land maps were still primitive, and the existing maps of Belgium didn't show anything except the rough positions of towns and villages and the roads that joined them. Sailors used sea charts, because they were much safer with them than without them; but landsmen were much less in the habit of visualising a bit of countryside from above, as it would be seen from say ten miles up in the sky. After all, it's not a natural point of view. They visualised it as they saw it, from their own eye-level. Once battle was joined, probably nobody would have bothered to look at those sketch maps anyway, but they would have been useful in the deployment that morning if there had been more copies; if Lord Uxbridge had had one, say, and the senior generals, and the staff. Now surely to goodness, if those maps were any good at all, and if they had been made some weeks before, they'd have taken the trouble to make a few more copies. I put it forward as a hypothesis, but a likely one, that it was only on the 16th, when the Duke rode past the cross-roads on the ridge, where the lane crossed the main road, and he saw the whole valley spread out in front of him, that he told de Lancey or some of his aides to ride along that lane in each direction and see where it led and what happened at the ends, and make a rough map

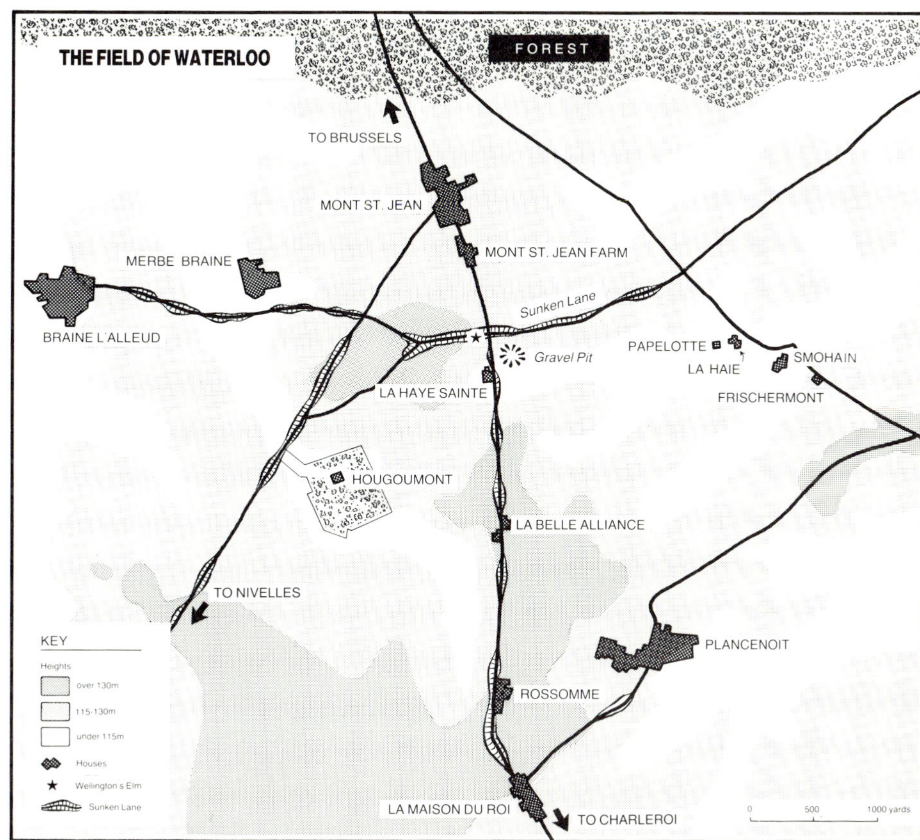

BELOW: Part of the *Carte de Cabinet* of the Austrian Netherlands drawn for the Count of Ferraris between 1771 and 1778 to a scale of approximately 1:27,000. This section shows the field of Waterloo in considerable detail.

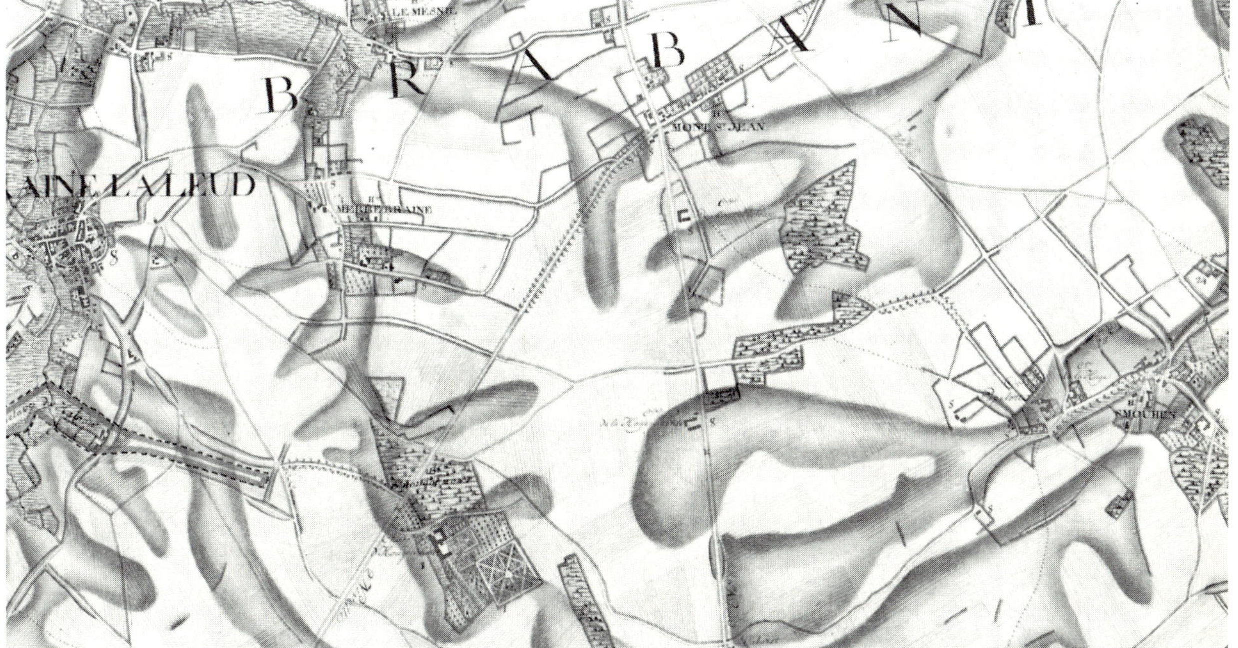

of what they saw. And it was then that they would have found the one weakness in the position, the valley that runs past Hougoumont.

Even when he had found and recognised the one conceivable place, he still doubted whether he could hold Napoleon there unless the Prussians could get there in time to help. The only alternative, in his eyes, was to fall back all the way, and abandon Brussels. At two o'clock in the morning of the 18th, the day of battle, that problem was still ahead of him – and that was almost the time when retreat, if it was to be retreat, would have to be ordered to give the army a chance of getting away. At almost the very last moment, an answer came from Marshal Blücher ten miles away across rough country to the east: his troops were exhausted, he himself was seventy-two years old and was still suffering from being rolled on by his horse and ridden over by two separate cavalry charges at Ligny – but he was coming as soon as he could. The Duke decided to stand and fight, and then went to bed and slept soundly for a couple of hours – which was all there was left of the night – in accordance with his confident precept, 'I make a point never to lie awake. It does no good.' And by six he had ridden down to Mont St Jean where Captain Gronow saw him with his glittering staff looking, he said (in one of his most felicitous phrases), as gay and unconcerned as if they were riding to meet the hounds in some quiet English county.

Blücher fallen from his horse at Ligny and ridden over by French cavalry.

It was when once battle was joined, or even some hours before it was joined, that Wellington's eye for the ground came into its own. I always used to wonder why there were five or six hours that morning when Wellington's army was ready and in position and Napoleon's was conspicuously not, and yet nothing happened. Wellington made no attempt to attack and catch Napoleon while he was still unorganised. I realise now that Wellington's eye had seen something Napoleon's eye had missed. That valley was a strong defensive position, but whichever way you came at it, whether from north or south, it was *only* a defensive position. Anybody who tried from either direction to attack across it was in for disaster. Indeed, the most notable thing about Waterloo was that Napoleon made three major attacks – and all three were disasters – while Wellington made only one, the British cavalry charge. That was a disaster as well. However, it was not ordered by Wellington but by Lord Uxbridge, who admitted at once he had made a ghastly mistake. And that is what's meant by an eye for the ground. You see not only the uses of the ground, but its limitations.

During those hours of waiting, the Duke rode down to Hougoumont. Here again, there's no indication that he'd ever been there before. He had been told about it, of course, and told also of the little valley it overlooks. That little valley begins, very shallow at first, quite near the main road at

La Papelotte farm today, on the left of the Waterloo position. The steepness of the slope down into 'the valley' may be judged from the levels of the buildings in this photograph.

La Belle Alliance, and growing gradually deeper and steeper it passes close under the walls of the stables and barn of Hougoumont, then begins to curve more to the north, crosses the Nivelles road and passes the end of the position the Duke had chosen. So it was a threat: troops in the bottom of it were in cover all the way, and could not be seen from the ridge. It was a ready-made route for a force to outflank the Duke. Of course he saw that it was, and saw also that the easiest, if not the only way, to plug it, was to put a strong and determined garrison in Hougoumont – which he had already done.

To do them justice, Napoleon's Marshals had seen it too, and Marshal Soult in particular urged the Emperor that morning to use it. But he adamantly refused, in very insulting terms, and insisted on a direct head-on attack across the main valley and up the ridge.

During those hours of waiting, also, Napoleon stood outside La Belle Alliance receiving the cheers of his troops as they marched up the road and deployed to each side along the southern edge of the valley. The Duke's army could plainly hear the cheering, the trumpets and drums and bands, and could plainly see the enemy, half a mile away across the valley – and Captain Kincaid of the Rifle Brigade wrote dourly, 'It looked as if they meant to scare us off the land.' The French also could plainly see the Duke's line of infantry on the skyline, still and silent – no cheering there, in fact they were rather bored and were asking each other the question soldiers through the centuries have asked each other, 'Why are we waiting?' Each army, in its own way, was indulging the ancient practice of displaying its strength to the other.

Then at last the French artillery went into action; and when the French infantry looked again, the Duke's line had gone. Well, I exaggerate a bit. There were still mounted officers on the ridge, still a few blocks of infantry or artillery on the forward slope. But there were wide gaps in the infantry line, where there had been none before. The greater part of it had vanished, and it did look to the French as if they had been successful in scaring it off the ground.

Now I must go back, and consider what the Duke had done and why he had done it, because this was the most famous example that day of his eye for the ground. And first I must offer a much closer look at the north side of the valley and the lane which runs along the edge of it. One speaks of that lane as running along a ridge, and so it does, but the ridge is so gentle and so low that you might almost walk along it without seeing it as a ridge at all. The importance of it is that from the bottom of the valley you can't see past the lane and over the ridge; you can't see what lies to the north of it.

Close to the cross-roads, where the lane crosses the main road, the virtues of the lane were obvious, because it ran in a cutting ten or fifteen feet deep, and provided a perfect lateral way where troops could move to right or left in safety. On the east of the main road, towards the left flank, the cutting is very short and runs out within a hundred yards or so. Beyond that, the lane was actually a few yards down the forward slope of the ridge, but there the lane had a hedge on each side of it, and so slight were the slopes of the ridge itself that the extra four or five feet of those hedges became an integral part of the battlefield. Behind the hedges the ground is practically level.

On the other side of the main road, towards the centre and right of the position, the cutting extended much further, a quarter of a mile or so. It doesn't now, because when the Netherlands government in the 1820's put up the enormous earthen pyramid with a lion on top in the middle of the Duke's front line, they dug away all the earth on the south side of the lane to a depth of ten feet, and so destroyed the central part of the battlefield they meant to commemorate. Along there on the north side of the lane you can still see the vestiges of the cutting, but on the south side, the important side, it's flat.

Beyond the end of the cutting, which was a bit before where the Lion Hill stands now, obstructing everything, the lane ran out into the open

Aerial view of the fields on which the Imperial Guard was defeated, showing the lack of cover, although not the lie of the contours. The 'battlefield architecture' in the foreground, including the mound and Belgian lion erected in the 1820s, has effectively obliterated some important features which it was designed to commemorate.

La Haye Sainte farmyard, looking west to the lion monument. The slope in the middle distance, leading up to the foot of the mound, is the area of the Imperial Guard's advance at the end of the battle.

again, very slightly on the north side of the ridge. This part of the field is still almost exactly as it was, except that the lane has been re-surfaced. That happened five or six years ago, when the motorway was being built round the north and west sides of the field, and the lane was used as part of a traffic diversion. You can still drive along it, which I think is a pity. But if you stand on the lane (and don't get run over) you can still see the lie of the land just as it was in 1815. You observe that to the south the sky-line (a fraction above your eye-level) is only fifty paces away, and you can't see beyond it and down to the bottom of the valley.

What the Duke did when the French artillery started was to order or permit a withdrawal of fifty or a hundred yards, behind the hedges on the left flank and the ridge itself on the right, and tell the troops to lie down.

I'm inclined to doubt if the Duke actually ordered this to be done. But still, a commander-in-chief gets the blame if anything goes wrong, so it's only fair he should get the credit if anything goes right – and this little movement went supremely right. It had the most astonishing effect on the whole of the battle.

I'm told the Duke had done the same thing in the Peninsula, and experts on the Peninsular War may confirm it. If so, he had set a precedent and put the idea into other people's minds – though I think the movement itself was so trivial that it would hardly have needed an order from the commander-in-chief. There was no possible danger in it. Nothing was going to happen suddenly. If the French advanced, they would be seen ten or fifteen minutes before they arrived: plenty of time to stand up again and reform the line. It looks as if Picton for one, out on the left where the hedges were, gave the order without referring it to the Duke; and I would guess that when the movement started anywhere it would spread, even perhaps by the soldiers shouting to their own officers, 'Look, sir, those so-and-so's are moving back and lying down. Why can't we? If we stand up here we'll all be killed.'

The explanation of the movement at the time was that there was some shelter from the artillery fire behind the ridge. Having looked at that ridge many times, not with the advantage of the Duke's eyes but with the advantage of hindsight, I doubt if the shelter was very real: the ridge is so low, and the trajectory of the French shot would have been falling at that range. I doubt therefore if there was more physical shelter behind the ridge than behind the hedges on the left. But there was psychological shelter, and that is important too. Old hands knew that artillery fire against an infantry line was more alarming than dangerous, and a man feels safer if the enemy can't see him. And lying down *would* have been a practical advantage. If a man lying down, with his head or his feet towards the enemy, presents a target a quarter the size, he has a quarter the risk of being hit.

That seems to have been the intention – shelter. But that small movement, the short retreat and the lying down, had another effect, and this is the one I find astonishing. Did it astonish the Duke? Or did he foresee it? I don't think anyone can ever know. But it deceived the French into thinking the line had gone, retreated in order or disorder, and left the ridge unguarded: and that led them to march straight into a trap.

They came first on the Duke's left, the east of the main road, with three solid blocks of infantry, 150 men in each rank and 24 ranks deep. I don't need to tell you why that was a useless formation, either for attack or defence; it was purely psychological, designed to look invincible, and I believe Napoleon's armies had used it successfully against less determined infantry. At Waterloo the first block of them came under fire from the Rifle Brigade, which was right on the crossroads. A bit further to their left, where the hedges were, the ridge still looked deserted, so the French infantry inclined right, and a few yards before the hedges they halted, and began the long complex manœuvre of deploying their formation into line. The only reason was the hedges: they were not very thick, and a man could force his way through almost anywhere, but a solid mass of men couldn't march through in formation. They still had no idea what the Duke had done –

that those hedges concealed an enemy – let alone the Gordons, the Black Watch, the Camerons and the First Royal Scots, and two or three hundred yards behind them the Union Brigade, 1,200 expert horsemen.

Through the Duke's trick – whether he foresaw it or not – the French remained unaware of all these men behind the hedges, until they were helpless in the middle of their deployment, when Picton shouted 'Fire' and the Scotsmen fired a volley of some 3,000 muskets into the mass of Frenchmen, and then broke through the hedges and charged with bayonets, followed by the cavalry who took the hedges like steeplechasers. Among the French, confusion, chaos, panic – and the remnants of them stumbled back if they could across the valley.

There's a strange resemblance between the battlefield of Waterloo and the battlefield of Hastings, over seven and a half centuries before. There's the valley, and the ridge to the north of it, and the main road which ran north and south across them both, and the lane at right angles on top of the ridge, and the shelter of forest to the rear. The Duke and King Harold even chose a similar place for their battle headquarters, just on the right of the main road and just in front of the lane. But King Harold stayed there all

La Haye Sainte, the 'Waterloo Farmhouse' on the Brussels–Charleroi road.

day – he was on foot of course – while the Duke rode to and fro all day right on top of the ridge, in front of his own troops, except for the moments at the height of the French cavalry attacks when everyone had to take refuge inside the infantry squares. The top of the ridge was dangerous, but it was the proper place for a commander-in-chief to be: by riding to right and left he could see everything that was going on and – which was just as important – his own men could see him, and his officers always knew where he was if they needed him.

It would have been superhuman if the Duke foresaw that the self-same trick would work not just once but three times over: superhuman because it depended on something he didn't know: that Napoleon was not in the proper place for a commander-in-chief. Most of the day, *he* was a mile back from his side of the valley, a mile and a half from the Duke's ridge, sitting with his elbows on his knees and his head in his hands in an old armchair which had been brought out for him from the farm of Rossomme. His staff who saw him there thought he was in a coma. The chair was said to have been on a little mound – I've never been able to discover which mound, but there is nowhere near Rossomme where you can see into the valley.

Wellington exercising his *coup d'œil* at Waterloo. This is obviously early in the day, since so many of his staff are still unwounded.

Marshal Ney, however, who you might say was the executive commander, was down in the bottom of the valley all day, fighting like a trooper, having five horses shot under him, breaking his sword, losing his cap and getting covered with mud. *Napoleon couldn't see into the valley, and Ney couldn't see out of it.* There were several excellent viewpoints near La Belle Alliance, but most of the day there was nobody there.

Now I hope I may make a slight digression. It is relevant to my theme to compare the two commanders-in-chief: the Duke, who displayed a remarkable eye for the ground, and the Emperor, who on that day displayed none whatever. The Emperor's absence back at Rossomme was certainly due to his misfortune in being a sick man on that important day, and people ever since have speculated what was wrong with him, until you would think there couldn't be anything more to say about it. But a short time ago I met a doctor, a specialist physician, who made a suggestion that was quite new to me. It may be an ancient hypothesis, and if so I apologise, but I'd never heard it before and I thought I'd pass it on in case it's also new to others.

It's generally agreed that the Emperor had an acute attack of piles: his brother Prince Jérôme revealed it long afterwards. Some French historians believe he also had an acute attack of cystitis, which he had often had before and which was revealed as a chronic condition in the post-mortem at St Helena. Both can be very painful: both together would have been worse than painful, and agonising if you also had to ride a horse all day.

But pain in itself does not explain all of Napoleon's behaviour in his final campaign. The most salient fact that his staff observed and reported was that on each of the three mornings of the campaign he was unable to concentrate his mind, to listen to anyone, to make decisions, or to give a coherent order. It happened on the morning of Ligny, again on the morning after Quatre Bras, and a third time on the morning of Waterloo. By each afternoon he was himself again, and led his battles with his usual skill: but only after a half of each day had been wasted.

Now the doctor believed this condition could only be caused by a drug. We know the Emperor's own prescription for piles was leeches (a most unpleasant thought) but that his physician Baron Larrey recommended what's usually translated as a 'lotion'. What could this lotion have been? Not, I am assured, an analgesic for exterior use, but only something given orally each evening to relieve the pain and let the patient sleep, and the most likely thing at that time was laudanum.

Not even the baron could have known the exact dose of a coarse preparation of laudanum to enable the Emperor to sleep and yet to wake up in the morning with all his faculties alert. The suggestion is that on each of those mornings he was fighting against a lingering overdose of laudanum. And this does indeed seem to be the only satisfactory explanation of the evident mental confusion that everybody noticed on those mornings, and of his recovery after the middle of each day.

RIGHT: The firebrand Marshal Ney, who must bear a significant share of the blame for defeat at Waterloo.

OVERLEAF TOP: Philippoteaux' epic painting shows none of the terror and pains of the Waterloo battlefield, but does clearly show the contours which were so vital to the tactics employed.

OVERLEAF BOTTOM: Napoleon reaping the bitter fruits of his torpor during the battle of Waterloo.

But in the afternoon of Waterloo, when he had recovered, he had another and better reason for staying back at Rossomme. The first of the Prussians had reached the village of Plançenoit, which is only a short mile east of Rossomme; and from there their artillery could threaten the main road in the rear of the French army. For a while around four o'clock that attack was much more of a menace than the Duke's passive defence. The Emperor had to give *that* his attention, and detach a force to push the Prussians back; which it did.

It was while he was preoccupied with pushing the Prussians back that the most extraordinary event of the day took place: the series of French attacks by massed cavalry. This happened to the right of the Duke's line, the part where the lane is just behind the ridge. His infantry were still lying down behind the crest, but the Duke among other mounted officers was on top, saw the cavalry coming, and was astonished. It was unheard of for cavalry to attack an infantry line alone, because the infantry had an almost impregnable defence against it: to form squares. Napoleon certainly didn't order it; in fact he knew nothing about it until he saw the horses a mile and a half away on the ridge, and refused to believe at first that they were his own. Ney didn't order it either, or not on anything like that scale. It simply grew, more and more people joining in, until the whole of the French cavalry were involved. The Duke could hardly believe it. He expected finesse from his famous opponent, and seemed disappointed: 'Dammit, the fellow's a mere pounder after all.' He gave the order 'Prepare to receive cavalry', and the infantry accordingly formed their squares, back on the lane where they had been lying. He let the cavalry come, and the simple trick he had played before worked again.

The infantry in their squares heard the horses coming, but they didn't see them until they came over the top fifty paces away. Until then, the cavalry didn't see the infantry either, and believed once more that the ridge was empty. Finding themselves under short-range fire of musketry and grape, they couldn't stop; you can't suddenly halt a mass of charging horses. They wouldn't give up, but kept on doing the same thing again and again, until those fifty paces between the lane and the ridge – you can see them now – were so encumbered with dead and dying horses and men that they couldn't again ride over them. They did a lot of damage too: the inside of some of the squares was said to be like a hospital or a morgue. But alone, without their infantry, they couldn't break the line.

And then the final attack by the Imperial Guard. In the French army an attack by the Guard was recognised as a prelude to victory, and this *was* ordered by the Emperor – indeed he came forward and led it himself a short distance down the main road into the valley. Some of his staff, knowing the day was lost, thought he ought to have led the attack; his brother Prince Jérôme, in particular, said he 'would never find a more glorious grave'. But he didn't look for it: he turned aside, and left to Ney the chance of honourable

One of the very best of the Wellington portraits, by Lawrence.

A British square at Quatre Bras; a flankless formation of infantry, four ranks deep, which presented a wall of bayonets and close-range fire that was impervious to cavalry.

death. Ney might have continued straight up the main road: there had certainly been a moment when the centre of the Duke's line was so weakened that the Guard might have marched right through to Brussels. But Ney didn't continue, nobody knows why: he turned off to the left, up the same long slope that the cavalry had churned into a bog. Perhaps he couldn't believe the cavalry had left a line intact up there.

Whatever the reason, the Duke was there, at the point on the ridge they were heading for, and he had instantly seen that there might be yet another chance for the same deception to work. He had re-formed the infantry from squares to a line four deep, and they were lying down again just behind the ridge, presumably among the dead horses. He stationed himself immediately behind the First Foot Guards: behind because the moment he gave the order there was going to be a ferocious short-range battle, and to be between the opponents was not the place for a commander-in-chief. And also because he could better judge from there the exact split second when to give the order. On horseback, he could see down the slope and into the valley: the infantry, lying down, could neither see nor be seen. He saw the Imperial Guard coming, and let them come. They began in more of a column than the infantry earlier in the day, but a very broad column, sixty men abreast. However, they lost their neat formation as they came through the mud and through the Duke's artillery fire. At the exact moment when his infantry saw the tall bearskin caps of the French Guard coming over the crest, he gave the order which has come down in history as 'Up, Guards and at 'em.' He always denied he said it, on the ground that he could only have given the men an order through their officers. A slightly more authoritative version is that he first shouted to their commanding officer, 'Now, Maitland! Now is your time.' And a few seconds later, perhaps because the action was not instantaneous, 'Up Guards! Make ready! Fire!' Whichever account is correct – if either – the effect was the same; a total surprise. No Frenchman in the leading ranks survived, but one from further back said graphically, 'They seemed to rise out of the ground.' The English remembered more clearly: the column, they said, seemed staggered, paralysed, convulsed. Again, it could not halt. The front ranks fell, and the ones behind piled into them. The Foot Guard charged with the bayonet, the slaughter was awful, and quite suddenly, the Imperial Guard's formation crumbled and they turned and ran. And all this had its origin in the Duke's eye for the ground.

The Imperial Guard on the run: the fatal news spread instantly through the Emperor's army, and in ten minutes reduced it – the finest army in the world – from an army to a rabble.

The Duke snapped his telescope shut and waved his hat, and the whole of his army left the ridge where it had stood all day, and poured down the slope in pursuit.

No victory has a single cause, and at Waterloo one can easily list half a dozen: the Emperor's ill-health, Ney's impetuosity, old Marshal Blücher's toughness and honesty, the Duke's utter calmness and presence of mind. And most important of all in any victory, the willingness and skill of n.c.o.'s and soldiers. And one must also add the Duke's eye for the ground, his knack of seeing the tactical importance of every tiny hill and valley, each wrinkle in the muddy field, many half-hidden under the crop of rye; which enabled him three times to deceive the French and beat off their three attacks. As we know, it was a near-run thing, 'the nearest run thing you ever saw in your life', he said. His eye for the ground didn't *win* the battle, but without it we may guess that the delicate balance would have been tilted, and the battle would have been lost.

CHAPTER 5

Under Fire: Wellington at Waterloo

JOHN KEEGAN

'Each captain, petty officer and man
Is only at his post when under fire'

– as Thomas Hardy makes Admiral Villeneuve say in Act V of *The Dynasts*. And indeed one of the cardinal ways in which naval differs from land warfare is that in action admirals and sailors alike are all in the same boat – in any sense of that much-imbued-with-meaning phrase. Villeneuve was not killed at Trafalgar, though he may very much have wished to die, and did perhaps commit suicide the following year. Nelson, of course, *was* killed – as, to cite the nearest recent example, it was wholly on the cards that Admiral Woodward might have been had his flagship been hit during the Falklands War. The list of admirals dying on their own quarterdecks is a long one, from Grenville at the Azores to Admiral Cradock at Coronel and Admiral Tom Phillips in the last action of the *Prince of Wales* and *Repulse* in 1942.

Generals, of course, have been killed in plenty, too. The list includes the Emperor Valens, slaughtered by the Goths at Adrianople in 378; Richard III, killed in the rout after Bosworth; and Stonewall Jackson, shot by mistake by one of his own men at Chancellorsville, but lingering long enough to utter what to me are the most beautiful of all recorded dying words – 'Let us cross over the river and rest under the shade of the trees.'

But dying is not, at least in our own time, regarded as one of the duties for which generals are appointed. Hitler raged against Paulus for choosing imprisonment instead of suicide after the surrender of Stalingrad in 1943, but he had unusual standards. There was, indeed, a powerful convention abroad throughout the years of civilised warfare – say from the beginning of the eighteenth century to the beginning of the twentieth – that an army had no business trying to kill commanders on the opposite side. 'How, if generals stooped to such depths', was the prevailing opinion, 'could they be expected to discharge their proper function – which was to execute the orders of their Sovereigns?'

But, if we ascend to an earlier moment in military history, we find altogether different standards applying. The Greeks of the heroic age had

Wellington riding down the *pavé* at Waterloo in the midst of his army. A reassuring image of warfare as it was perceived in the 1890s.

no doubt that the right place for the leader was not merely in the centre of the battle line but actually in front of it, as we read so graphically described in Homer's account of the duel between Hector and Achilles under the walls of Troy. Xenophon, a figure of history rather than myth, actually raised the question of the generals' proper status, and decided that, given the choice to display bravery or practise reflection, the general must choose to be brave, since everything turned upon his example.

And then, suddenly, there was a change of view. Philo of Byzantium, writing in the third century BC at a time when drill and formation had recently become more complex, records that there has been a revolution in attitude. His advice to a general reads as follows:

> It is your duty *not* to take part in the battle, for whatever you may accomplish by spilling your own blood could not compare with the harm you could do to your interests as a whole if anything happened to you.... Keeping yourself out of range of missiles, or moving along the lines without exposing yourself, exhort the soldiers, distribute praise and honour to those who prove their courage and berate and punish the cowards.

His advice would not always be taken. Indeed we know from Caesar's account of his own conduct at the Battle against the Nervii on the Sambre in 57 BC that, at a moment of crisis, he felt it imperative to seize shield and sword and plunge into the thick of the fight – an impulse which has come to many generals since, not least to John Terraine's hero Haig, who, at the crisis of the 1st Battle of Ypres in 1914, mounted his horse and rode out up the Menin Road to seek death – should it come to him – if that were the means of inspiring his men to a final supreme effort.

These examples to the contrary (and the heroic leaders of the wars of the Middle Ages would also think it necessary to behave like Achilles and Hector rather than the calculating military functionaries whom Philo of Byzantium held up as an example), generalship unquestionably underwent a decisive change in later classical times, which provided a typecast for generalship in the era of organised warfare from the Renaissance onwards. Once armies became paid and permanent, their commanders' time and energies had to be devoted to their management rather than to their inspiration – to *command* rather than leadership.

Napoleon's own style is an object lesson in this transformation. As a young general with a reputation to make, he was ready to put himself in the front rank, as he did in the famous assault on the bridge at Lodi in the Italian campaign of 1796. By the time of Austerlitz, in 1805, he was content to leave the direction of the battle – after he had master-minded its strategic antecedents – to his staff. And at Waterloo, as we know, he chose – with fatal results – to devolve command on to Ney who, behaving as if Philo of Byzantium had never written (it is wholly incredible, of course, that he had ever read him) led several cavalry charges and persisted, in the closing stages of the day, in trying to get himself killed.

Getting himself killed was never at any time in his career on Wellington's agenda. It smacked of a theatricality quite alien to his nature. But, too often, he had less choice in the matter than was ideal. After all, Wellington was a specialist in making a little go a long way and had therefore survived a large number of small battles. He had had a horse killed under him at Assaye in 1803. He had been nearly killed at point blank range by French musketry while on reconnaissance before Talavera in 1809. His holster and cloak were penetrated by a bullet at Salamanca in 1812. He had to ride for his life only two days before Waterloo at Quatre Bras, when he had jumped the bayonets of his own infantry, the 92nd, to get away from pursuing French cavalry. But that was in the nature of things – of the way he was obliged to fight. With small armies under command, they had to be spread thin; and, being spread thin, their commander was necessarily pushed close to the firing line even while remaining behind it.

With so much exposure to this sort of experience, Wellington no doubt expected to feel the breath of danger at Waterloo – if, that is, he had any emotional room for such an anxiety, which is unlikely. For one thing, almost all officers testify that responsibility dissolves concern for personal safety to an almost magical degree, and the greater the responsibility the more effectively. But, for another, Wellington must already have been fairly anaesthetised by the exertions of the previous days.

If we follow Wellington's itinerary and routine in the three days before the battle, Thursday 15th June to Saturday 17th June, it runs something like this: he rose early on 15th June at Brussels, and got to bed at 2 am the following morning, 16th June – this, of course, was the night of the Duchess of Richmond's ball. He rose at 5.30 am on 16th June at Brussels and left, after tea and toast, to ride the twenty-two miles to Quatre Bras. He commanded the battle all day and got to bed at Genappe (in the *Roi d'Espagne* inn) at midnight. He rose again at 3 am on the morning of 17th June, and rode back the three miles to Quatre Bras. He directed the retreat all day and got to bed at Waterloo, about twelve miles away, between 11 and 12 that night. He rose on the morning of 18th June at 3 am, wrote letters, and was seen by Lieutenant Drewe of the Inniskilling Fusiliers watching the troops march up to the battlefield, from the balcony of his lodging, before six o'clock. If we tot this up, therefore, we find that Wellington had had no more than nine and a half hours sleep in three nights, had ridden at least ten miles a day, had fought a battle, been in danger of his life and overseen a retreat. He had, it is true, had a little snooze on the afternoon of the 17th, when he lay down in his cloak by the side of the road with a copy of the *Sun* newspaper over his face. But, averaging it out, between the mornings of 15th and 18th, he had been awake for sixty-three hours and slept for less than ten.

Wellington's attachment to his camp bed, even during his time as Prime Minister, is here satirised by the press, 1829.

Great as his resilience was, tiredness must have been operating to palliate the flutterings of any personal fear he may have had – and also to steady

Wellington's headquarters in the hamlet of Waterloo – today commercialised and transformed into a museum.

and channel his anxieties as a commander. Field Marshal Slim, describing his own reaction to crisis during the early days of the campaign against the Japanese in Burma, spoke of the 'sinking of the heart as each fresh piece of bad news came in – followed by the glow of resolution as the mind grappled with the problem – to be succeeded by the thrill of exhilaration as I recognised that it could be contained and manipulated to my ends'. We may suppose that Wellington was experiencing something of the same succession of feelings.

All generals depend upon their subordinates in time of crisis for moral as well as functional support – but Wellington less so than most. To an inordinate degree, the Duke was a man of composure and self-control to whom the personality of others was almost a matter of indifference. Nevertheless, he had been glad to get rid of his chief staff officer, Sir Hudson Lowe, Napoleon's future gaoler, before Waterloo. 'As for Lowe', he said later in

Writing the Waterloo despatch, in cramped and crowded quarters at the culminating point of many sleepless days and nights. It is scarcely surprising if this and other comparable documents tell the historian rather less than he would ideally wish to know.

private conversation, 'he is a damned fool. When I came to Brussels from Vienna in 1815, I presently found the damned fellow would instruct me in the equipment of the army, always producing the Prussians to me as models. I was obliged to tell him I had commanded a much larger army in the field than any Prussian general, and that I was not to learn from their service how to equip an army. I thought this would have stopped him, but shortly afterwards he was at me again. I was obliged to write home and complain; the Government were kind enough to take him away from me.' In his place Wellington was pleased to have got Sir William De Lancey, reckoned the second most able man in the army for the position of Q.M.G. The ablest, Murray, was in America. De Lancey headed a personal staff of thirty-three, of whom thirty-one had served in the Peninsula.

But ultimately Wellington would command the army himself. He had always done far more than his fair share of the work of the staff, partly out of objective recognition of his own superiority in every branch of military staff work, partly out of an obsessive element in his character which would trust to no one what he felt he could do best himself.

Let us find him now, at six in the morning of the battle, watching his troops march up to the front. He has been up, we know, since three o'clock, has been writing letters – one, curiously, to a personal friend, Lady Frances Webster, in London. His state of mind was calm – 'I will give you the earliest information of any danger that may come to my knowledge, at present I know of none,' he had told her – and shortly afterwards he mounted Copenhagen, his chestnut charger, which had carried him at Vitoria, the Pyrenees and Toulouse, and rode off towards Mont St Jean. As he left he received Blücher's assurance that the Prussian Army was coming to his assistance.

The battle which was about to begin, we now know, would divide into five main phases – something Wellington certainly could not foresee. The first would be the French attack on the *château* of Hougoumont, the second d'Erlon's infantry assault in the centre, repulsed by Wellington's infantry and then routed by British cavalry charges; the third would be the great cavalry battle of the afternoon, when charge after charge would break on the British squares lining the ridge between the crossroads and Hougoumont; the fourth would be the French success in the centre, culminating in the capture of La Haye Sainte; the fifth and final episode was to be the advance of the Imperial Guard on the right, and its devastation by the British infantry.

I say Wellington could not foresee this sequence of events. But he did, nevertheless, help to pre-determine the course of events by what he did in the first hours on the field – which was to lay out his troops. This was not done *entirely* by *coup d'oeil* – or off the cuff, as we might say nowadays. He had seen the field in August 1814, as we know, and he had had a rough map of it since Quatre Bras, hastily pieced together by the Royal Engineer Brigade Major at Brussels from sketches made by engineer officers and brought to Wellington by Lieutenant Waters, RE, on the Quatre Bras battlefield. The map can still be seen in the Royal Engineers Museum at Chatham; faintly visible on it are some pencil marks made by Wellington during the fighting at Quatre Bras which indicate where he had already planned to position his men should he have to fight at Waterloo.

They had been approximately positioned the night before. He now rode out to make detailed adjustments. As we know, the battlefield is about two miles wide, and divides obviously into three sections. East of the Brussels–Charleroi Road it is encumbered by a collection of small villages called Papelotte, Smohain and La Haye, the ground behind which was held by Hanoverians with British cavalry in support. As far as we know, Wellington did not visit this part of the field at all, either before or during the battle. West of the Brussels–Charleroi Road the field becomes open, sloping down

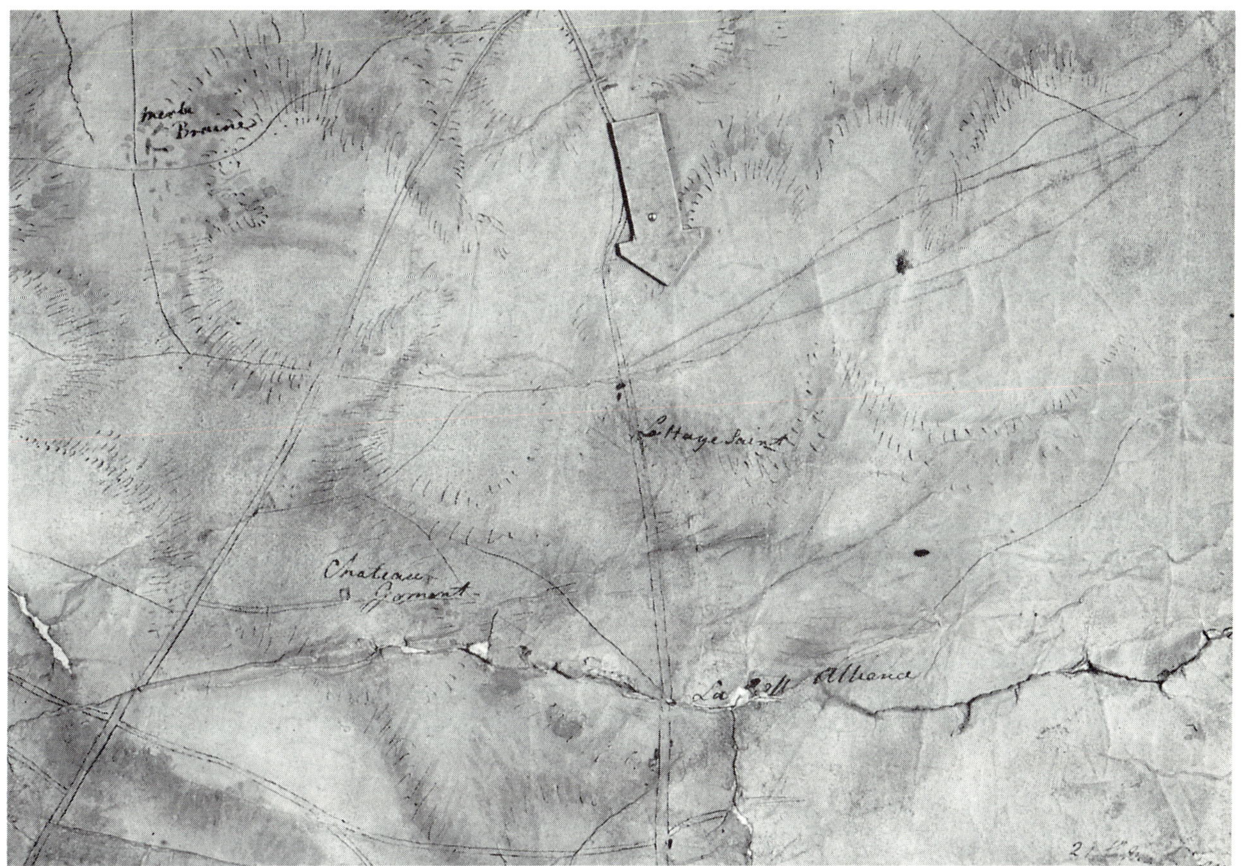

Detail from the Chatham map. This map covers an area some twelve miles across, including the Waterloo battle site. It was sketched by Royal Engineers before the opening of the campaign, under the direction of Lieutenant Colonel James Carmichael-Smyth CRE. Wellington marked his positions for the battle upon it in pencil on 17th June, and the following day it was found on the person of his Chief of Staff, de Lancy, when he was mortally wounded.

to the ridge on which the French were drawn up – Wellington could undoubtedly see the French massed in review order for Napoleon's inspection, as soon as he arrived on the crest of his own ridge. And at the far end of the field, orchards connect the spur with the advanced strongpoint of Hougoumont farm and *château*. Later in the morning the Duke passed by the buildings, noting the measures taken for their defence, but did not go in. They were held by the light companies of the Footguards in whom he had perfect confidence.

His radius of action, therefore, ran between the crossroads on the Charleroi–Brussels road, where it was crossed by what was then a farm track and where a latterly famous elm tree stood, and the end of the ridge above Hougoumont – a distance of about three-quarters of a mile – over which he was to ride constantly throughout the day, always present where danger pressed most urgently and therefore shot flew thickest.

He began the day, however, far out on the right flank, west but north of Hougoumont, where he had gone to chivvy some Nassauers – allied troops – into line. They were having breakfast, were not keen for action, answered his promptings to get into line by packing up and making off and when he

A somewhat stylised and geometrical thunderstorm on the eve of Waterloo, as imagined by William Heath.

persisted some of them actually fired on him – luckily it was at long range and they were no sharper shots than they were soldiers. 'Did you see those fellows run?', he asked the Austrian officer on his staff, with good-humoured contempt. It is just possible they did not know who he was, or why he was so keen to expose them to the enemy's fire, because he was, as usual in action, dressed as a civilian – in white buckskin breeches, a blue frock coat, a cocked hat, and a blue cloak – which he put on or off, he recalled, fifty times that day. Sunday 18th June was overcast, though hot, with frequent short showers of rain. The weather would do much to thicken up the atmosphere on the battlefield, over which visibility would shorten very rapidly as soon as cannon and muskets began to discharge their dense clouds of white or grey smoke.

And here, of course, we have one more explanation of Wellington's behaviour under fire that day. His experience, and his personal preference, drove him to command in person rather than through his staff – which, we

The damp and uncomfortable awakening on the misty morning of the battle.

can see with hindsight, was not yet of a sort on to which command authority could be devolved. But physically it was actually necessary for Wellington to be close up if he was to see what was going on. Prevailing visibilities are difficult to reconstruct in retrospect. Quite good at the start of the day – he could see to the far skyline, we know – by the late afternoon they had come down to a few hundred yards. We do know that at six o'clock, when La Haye Sainte was lost, he could not see the light infantry of the K.G.L. leaving the farm buildings from his station at the crossroads even though the distance between the two points is only about two hundred and fifty yards.

However, visibility was still good at the opening moment, about 11.25 (some say 11.50) when the French cannonade opened. At this time, Wellington was behind Hougoumont, on the high ground, looking out across the valley at the grand battery of the French artillery seven hundred yards away. His first order was to his staff to disperse – 'you are too thick on the ground' is his reputed remark – and he then began to issue orders for the conduct of the fighting. His means of doing so were partly by word of mouth, to his ADCs or other staff officers – the assistant and deputy assistant QMGs and AGs – partly by written order. I think we must all agree that the most fascinating of the items exhibited at Apsley House – the most fascinating to me of all military documents, by which I have been mesmerised since I first saw it as a schoolboy – are the slips of asses' skin on which he wrote his orders, using a soft lead pencil – and in remarkably legible handwriting, rather reminiscent in style of the strong and beautifully orthography of Dr Johnson.

As the cannonade rose in intensity – Wellington was well within its range – Jérôme's division came forward to begin the assault on Hougoumont, and at that time the Duke was in the open, a little north-east of Hougoumont, to keep the situation under observation. He repositioned Bull's battery of 5.5 inch howitzers, the better to bring the advancing columns of French infantry under fire with explosive or shrapnel shell. He also withdrew such Nassauers as had stayed – he had good reason to doubt their reliability – and brought du Plat's brigade of the K.G.L. – utterly steady soldiers – up behind Hougoumont in their place. He kept under his hand the main body of the Guards Brigade, which were to be his reserve during this stage of the battle.

A contemporary (1816) print, showing the inferno at Hougoumont in a manner which could not be mistaken or forgotten.

It swayed back and forth; the orchard fell. Wellington sent down four companies of Coldstreamers, who attacked and recaptured the orchard. The French then shifted their effort to the buildings themselves and Lieutenant Legros, *l'enfonceur*, broke down the main door with an axe seized from one of his pioneers. While fighting raged within the courtyard, the Duke despatched another four companies of Coldstreamers, who helped the garrison to trap the French assault party inside the courtyard, a terrible episode in which every Frenchman who had got in, except a drummer boy, was hunted down and killed. A further crisis in the orchard was resolved when Wellington released two companies of the Scots Guards, who skirmished through the hedges and drove the French survivors away again.

His local reserve was now almost exhausted, but the situation was stabilised. The most alarming development was not a tactical one. A French shell had set fire to the buildings and threatened to drive the British out, willy-nilly. It was at this time, probably near one o'clock, that Wellington pencilled the best known of his notes:

> I see that the fire has communicated from the hay stack to the roof of the *Château*. You must, however, still keep your men in those parts to which the fire does not reach. Take care that no men are lost by the falling in of the roof, or floors. After they will have fallen in [notice the use of the future perfect], occupy the ruined walls inside of the garden, particularly if it should be possible [future subjunctive] for the enemy to pass through the embers in the inside of the House.

I would be pleased with myself had I written such prose in the solitude of my study.

Wellington's hurried note to the garrison of Hougoumont at the height of the battle: as perfect an example as one could wish of his prose style.

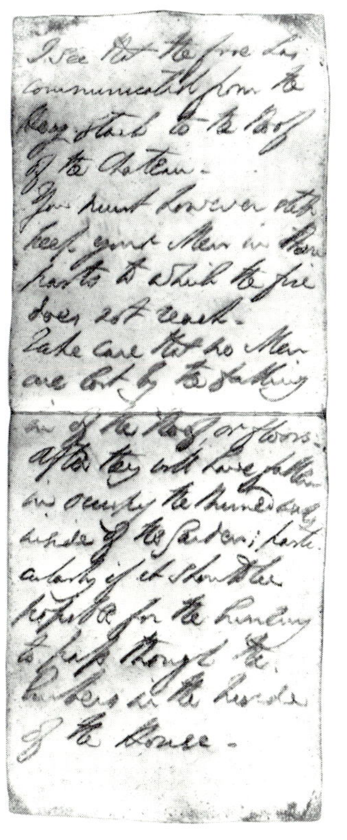

I see that the fire has
communicated from the
hay stack to the Roof
of the Chateau.
You must however still
keep your Men in those
parts to which the fire
does not reach.
Take care that no Men
are lost by the falling
in of the Roof or floors.
after they will have fallen
in occupy the Ruined walls
inside of the Garden; particularly if it should be
possible for the Enemy
to pass through the
Embers in the inside
of the House.

At about 1.30 Wellington left the ground behind Hougoumont and made his way eastward to his elm, where Bijlandt's unfortunate Belgians were standing out forward of the ridge, under intense French artillery fire, preparatory to the launch of d'Erlon's mass infantry assault. Wellington rode forward to the Sandpit on the Charleroi road held by the 1/95th Rifles to get a closer look, and then, as he saw that the dense columns of d'Erlon's corps, 18,000 strong, had started forward from a line of departure about 1,200 yards to the south, he returned to the elm to direct the defence. He had summoned reinforcements and could now only wait for fire-power to defeat fire-power.

He had a sudden local crisis to deal with when some French cuirassiers, riding in support, overran a Hanoverian battalion; which he righted by bringing two fresh brigades forward. Otherwise, he could only really watch and pray at this moment – and it was now precisely that one of the few mistaken orders of the battle was given – not by the Duke but by his cavalry commander, Uxbridge, who, as d'Erlon's men reeled under the British musketry and began to break, released the Union Brigade to follow them, with results initially damaging to the French but ultimately more destructive to the British horsemen.

In the aftermath of d'Erlon's attack, Wellington was much about the centre of the battlefield, going forward as far as the Sandpit again, to see the 1/95th back into position, and then hurrying battalions forward to thicken up the line. It was swiftly clear, however, that the crisis was shifting from the immediate centre to the centre-right, where his young British infantry battalions were lining the ridge. Leaving his elm tree, therefore, the Duke went westward. We may guess that the time was about three o'clock. The next hour and a half was both the busiest and most dangerous passage of the battle for the Duke. The French cavalry advancing in thick waves of regiments, some of which charged as many as twelve times that afternoon, boiled against and round the British squares, threatening the integrity of the line, which in places and at times they actually penetrated. Wellington was here, there and everywhere. Occasionally he popped into a square, the men opening ranks to let him in, and sat the charge out, uttering brief words of encouragement the while. More often, he 'relied on his own dexterity as a horseman and the speed of his horse' to escape when danger threatened. About 4.30 he heard the first sound of cannon from the south-east, bringing the reassuring knowledge that the Prussians were indeed coming to his rescue and that he had only to sustain the defence a little longer for the course of the battle to be decisively altered.

PREVIOUS PAGES: An over-animated vision of cavalry – hooves not touching the ground – meeting unconcerned infantry firing – apparently – lilliputian carbines.

About 5.30, after he had brought forward Adam's brigade of veteran British infantry, the last French cavalry attack petered out, and he could leave the centre-right to return to his elm where a new crisis had developed. That was around La Haye Sainte, the K.G.L.'s advanced strongpoint on the Charleroi–Brussels road. It had come under strong infantry attack and, unknown to the Duke, its garrison of the 2nd Light Bn, K.G.L., was running out of ammunition. To his chagrin – an observer noted that he looked 'much vexed' – he saw, about six o'clock, the Second Battalion and the reinforcement of the First Light Battalion, K.G.L., streaming back through the smoke from the building which they had had to abandon.

No time to repine. The main position in the centre was still firm, but a massive threat now loomed on the right. It is said that a French cavalry officer was the first to warn of it. Wellington's battlefield sense, and silent computation of what Napoleon had left by way of reserves, probably reinforced any formal warning he got; the Imperial Guard was on its way.

He appears, at this point, to have ridden right across the line as far as the high ground above Hougoumont, then back along the line to check its strength and reposition units and then finally back – in all a ten-minute ride – to the west again, from which spot he was to direct the British resolution of the crisis of the battle.

It occurred about eight o'clock. The Imperial Guard came forward in thick columns, attempting to deploy into line as they reached musket shot of the British line, formed at that point by the Guards Brigade. They were about forty yards distant and a curious silence had fallen on the ridge at that point. In it the Duke's voice was heard calling, 'Now, Maitland, now's your time.' Then, 'Stand up Guards. Make ready. Fire.' As the front ranks of the French stood inert under the volley which followed, the rear of their formation, impelled by psychic tremors telling them all was up, turned and broke back towards their own front. As they began to make off, Colborne's 1/52nd, whom Wellington had ordered up moments before, wheeled into line on their flank and completed the disintegration.

Wellington rode forward. His battlefield instinct told him the battle was won. Two of his ADCs begged him to keep back for fear of falling at the last moment, and he answered, 'So I will when I see these fellows driven off.' To his soldiers he called – with the certain insight of a supremely experienced veteran – 'Well done, Colborne ... go on, go on. Don't give them time to rally. *They won't stand.*'

The day under fire was nearly over. But he still rode forward, following his men as they pursued the French southward. One of his staff officers, Felton Hervey, begged him again not to take such risks, among the final

Hillingford's late nineteenth-century impression of General Hill's summons to the Imperial Guard to surrender, towards the end of the battle of Waterloo.

skirmishes of the rout. 'We are getting into enclosed ground,' he said, 'and your life is too valuable to be thrown away.' 'Never mind,' he answered, 'let them fire away. The battle's won; and my life is of no consequence *now*.' (I like that '*now*'.)

Wellington offering consolation to the Marquess of Anglesey on the occasion of the loss of his leg at Waterloo.

A little later at about nine o'clock, he met Blücher outside La Belle Alliance and was kissed by the old Prussian, who was smelling as usual strongly of rhubarb and liniment. They spoke in French, their only common language. Then the Duke turned to ride back to his lodging of the morning, took supper, and soon after midnight fell asleep. He slept on a pallet on the floor since he had given his bed to his QMG, De Lancey, who was dying of wounds.

Wellington had not been touched. That he had been spared was unquestionably one of the most remarkable outcomes of the battle, for he had been exposed to danger from its beginning to its end. Of his personal staff of sixty-three, no less than twenty had been killed or wounded – casualty figures of thirty per cent, a ratio higher than that suffered by the fighting soldiers themselves. Moreover, he himself had consistently been within cannon range of the enemy and frequently within musket range – say a hundred yards. That he had been mobile only made his exposure more extreme, for he always moved *towards* not *away* from fire.

His conduct thus transgressed the rules of modern post-heroic generalship, which Philo of Byzantium had laid down 2,000 years before. He had behaved like Alexander the Great, riding at the head of his men to capture the Emperor Darius – while Napoleon had not behaved even as Caesar had done in the crisis of the battle against the Nervii. I have no hesitation, when the inevitable arguments arise about the comparative greatness of the two as generals, in casting my pebble into the pot for Wellington. At Waterloo, as supreme a crisis for his cause as it was for Napoleon's own, he spared nothing – thought, preparation, energy, personal safety – to make sure that his army put forth all it could. Napoleon, who I do not think ever at any of his battles achieved a similar level of exertion, made no attempt to go even the first mile with Wellington at Waterloo, and deservedly lost.

Moreover, in a curious anticipatory comment on later generalship, it was Napoleon's example which was to furnish the style for the First World War generals – and it was also that style which was to be rejected by their successors in the Second World War. Napoleon, in fact, had forgotten – whatever Philo of Byzantium might have written – that bravery and example are crucial and central elements of leadership; a perception which stood at the centre of Wellington's approach to command. Wellington must, therefore, be seen not merely as a hero, but also as a man of the future. He is, of all figures of the past, among those whom I most admire and would most keenly like to meet, if only to have my eyes damned as one of those fools who thinks he can 'write the history of a battle'.

CHAPTER 6

Playing Into Wellington's Hands – Bonaparte's Mistakes

CORRELLI BARNETT

It was originally suggested that this paper should discuss 'Wellington's exploitation of Bonaparte's[1] mistakes'; but that doesn't entirely cover the reality. The Duke himself remarked to Fitzroy Somerset on 15th June that there was no doubt about him defeating Bonaparte 'provided I do not make a false Movement'. Then there is the famous exchange with Uxbridge, when Uxbridge asked the Duke's plans for the day of Waterloo, and the Duke asked him: 'Who will attack first tomorrow, I or Bonaparte?' 'Bonaparte'. 'Well, Bonaparte has not given me any idea of his projects; and as my plans will depend on his, how can you expect me to tell you what mine are?'

The salient fact was that Bonaparte seized and held the military initiative from the beginning of the campaign until finally repulsed on the field; and that Wellington's and Blücher's conduct could only be reactive. Bonaparte enjoyed this initiative partly because of his own skill in mystifying the allied commanders as to his main thrust-line; partly because he headed an army of veteran soldiers, while Wellington led a polyglot army partly composed of very raw soldiers indeed. There could be no question of Wellington trying for a Salamanca or a Vitoria; it had to be a cautious, waiting game that gave as few openings as possible for Bonaparte's favourite trick of pugilistic opportunism. Therefore Wellington could not 'exploit Bonaparte's mistakes'; he could only encourage Bonaparte to make mistakes by presenting him with as subtle and staunch a defensive as possible. It is in this sense, then, that I will discuss the campaign.

But what is, I think, legitimate is to compare Wellington's handling of Bonaparte's characteristic attempt to wrong-foot and rout an enemy by sheer aggressive bustling, with that of previous opponents of Bonaparte. For I have always been struck by the nature of the Waterloo campaign as a *reprise*, or repay, of Bonaparte's earlier campaigns and earlier mistakes, as I shall hope to show. It would be wrong, however, to limit such a comparison to the purely military events of the campaign. Dare I say it, but there is a tendency in an older school of military historians to see campaigns and

Napoleon in 1812 by one of his admirers, Lefevre.

battles in the nature of games – like test matches or Wimbledon – fought for a silver cup called 'Victory', and where it is the military historian's job to analyse the foot-work and stroke-play, and award merit marks or demerit marks. The Waterloo campaign itself is such a colossal drama – the Hundred Days, the final rout of Bonaparte – that it particularly attracts this sort of treatment: war as a game. Never let Clausewitz' dictum be forgotten that war is a political activity, conducted throughout for political objectives, with the actual military aspects always lying within a political framework. So it was with the Waterloo campaign. Wellington himself had played a key role in creating the right political framework – not as a general, but as a statesman; as British delegate to the Congress of Vienna at the time of Bonaparte's escape from Elba. He took a leading part in the negotiation of a formal alliance between the allied powers – Britain, Russia, Prussia and Austria – to defeat and re-imprison Bonaparte; likewise in framing the grand strategy by which up to a million allied soldiers were eventually to invade France on a broad front from Flanders to the Swiss frontier – and keep moving relentlessly towards Paris no matter what local rebuffs Bonaparte might inflict. In other words, the strategy of protracted war, of attrition, which had brought victory in the campaigns of 1813 and 1814 – the one strategy necessarily fatal to a gambler on narrow margins like Bonaparte.

Now this rock-hard political alliance and concerted allied strategy constituted the essential precondition for the successful conduct of the war itself. As Bismarck understood in 1866 and 1870, you must get the political frame for a war right first. In 1815 the allied policy agreed in Vienna by Wellington and his colleagues ensured that Bonaparte could not win on the political plane, because his only hope of success lay in splitting the coalition by a quick victory in the field. I see this as the first and basic example of Wellington and the other allies encouraging Bonaparte to make his own ultimately fatal mistakes.

This brings me to a comparison between the opening of the Waterloo campaign, Bonaparte's last, and the opening of his first – the Italian campaign of 1796; a comparison which illustrates the importance of the political framework of war. In 1815 Bonaparte proposed to strike at the junction between Wellington's army and Blücher's, and drive Blücher eastwards away from Wellington. He would then concentrate against Wellington, smash him, enter Brussels and end the campaign. In 1796 the pattern had been curiously similar. Bonaparte likewise intended to strike at the junction of two allied armies, the Piedmontese and Austrian. He likewise intended to defeat one of them, the Austrian, and drive it away to the east, so that he could then smash the Piedmontese and march on their capital Turin. He did in fact defeat the Austrians; he did then turn on the Piedmontese. And after an action or two the Piedmontese sued for an armistice, and the campaign was over. According to the Bonapartian version of history, this was a brilliant strategic victory. But in fact the Austrians did not retreat away

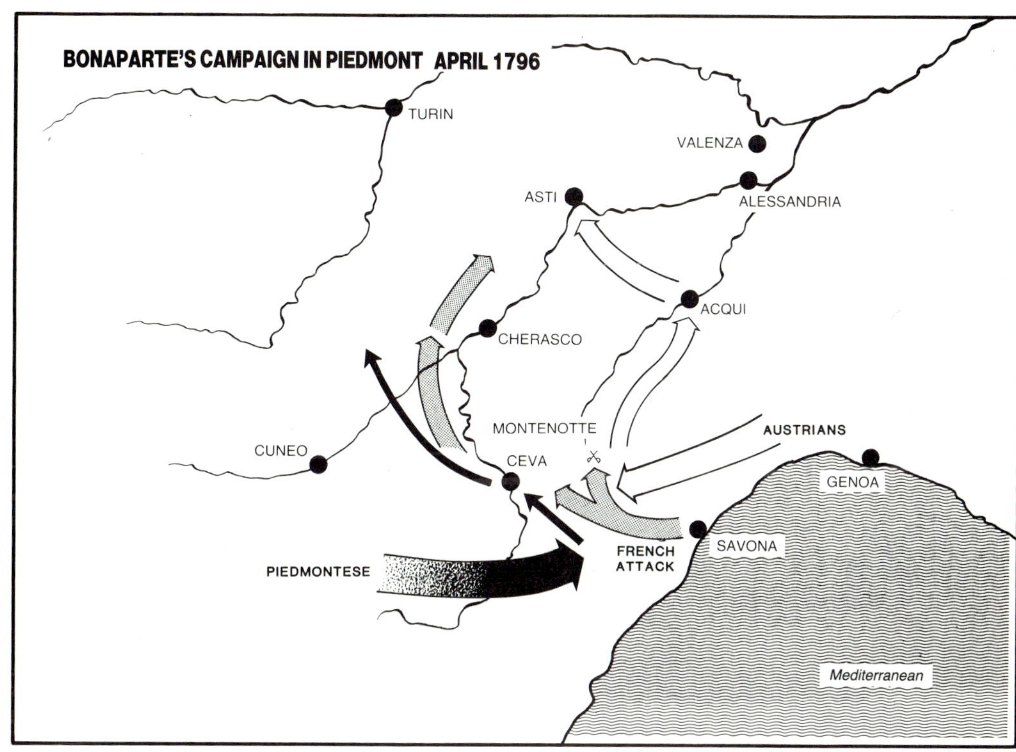
BONAPARTE'S CAMPAIGN IN PIEDMONT APRIL 1796
TURIN
VALENZA
ASTI
ALESSANDRIA
ACQUI
CHERASCO
MONTENOTTE
AUSTRIANS
CUNEO
CEVA
GENOA
SAVONA
FRENCH ATTACK
PIEDMONTESE
Mediterranean

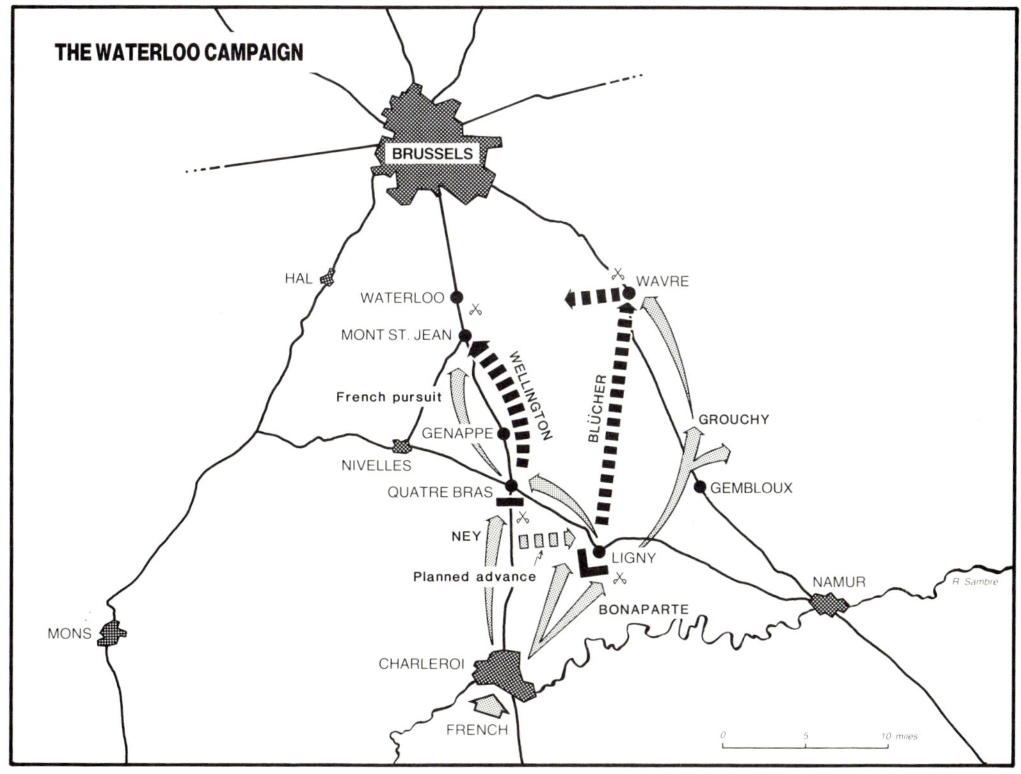
THE WATERLOO CAMPAIGN
BRUSSELS
HAL
WATERLOO
WAVRE
MONT ST. JEAN
WELLINGTON
BLÜCHER
French pursuit
GROUCHY
GENAPPE
NIVELLES
QUATRE BRAS
GEMBLOUX
NEY
LIGNY
Planned advance
NAMUR
R. Sambre
BONAPARTE
MONS
CHARLEROI
FRENCH
0 5 10 miles

A French bivouac, or rather 'shanty town' might be a better description. The French made a virtue of their improvisations in such matters, which is another way of saying that they lacked system and regulation.

from their allies, but northwestwards to re-join them. And in fact, again, the Piedmontese did not ask for an armistice because they had been crushed in the field by Bonaparte, but because a long-standing peace party at the Piedmontese court used Bonaparte's rather hollow successes to sway the argument in their favour.

But what happened in 1815? Again Bonaparte attacked one allied army, in this case the Prussian, and defeated it at Ligny. Again he thought he had succeeded in driving it away from the other allied army, in this case Wellington's. But in fact Blücher retreated northwards on a parallel route to Wellington's own retirement, in order to link up later – just like the Austrians in Italy in 1796. But this time the allied armies did actually link up again – on the field of Waterloo – and fought a united battle that smashed Bonaparte's army. They were able to do so because there was no effective peace party in any allied court in 1815 that could betray the generals in the field. Because, indeed, Wellington himself was a member of the British political establishment. So there was no chance that Bonaparte's enemies would play into his hands in 1815 as they had in 1796. Here was a basic Bonapartian miscalculation. The allies had got the political fundamentals of their war right before the actual campaign opened; Bonaparte had got them wrong. Could you call this the exploitation of a mistake?

Now I come to the campaign itself. Those historians who start from the premise that Bonaparte was a brilliant genius try to argue that since he lost the campaign it must be that he was off form, let down by his subordinates, and that all in all this was not a typical Bonaparte performance. I totally disagree with this view. I see the Waterloo campaign as a quite characteristic and average Bonapartian exercise, with various parallels with previous exercises. What was different this time was that he was up against Wellington, and not against bumbling idiots like General Mack at Ulm in 1805 or the *committee* of bumbling idiots who commanded the allied armies at Austerlitz. And remember that old Blücher, though no original thinker, was a fighter through and through.

Let's start with the day of Quatre Bras and Ligny – with Bonaparte's attempt to hold off Wellington while he concentrated against Blücher. Remember that Bonaparte could field only some 128,000 men (including 22,300 cavalry) and 344 guns, against an allied total in Belgium of over 200,000 men and nearly 500 guns. He therefore needed, if possible, to defeat Blücher and Wellington separately and one at a time. He also needed to get every available man into action.

Bonaparte's first self-inflicted wound on the day of Quatre Bras and Ligny was to leave an entire army corps (Lobau's) idle back at Charleroi for want of orders – over 10,000 men, a twelfth of his total strength. Do we see here a sign that the Bonaparte of 1815 was no longer on the ball? Not at all: to leave major formations out of a battle for want of orders, or because of late orders, or badly drafted orders, was common form with Bonaparte, as I shall discuss. The nearest parallel to his leaving Lobau's corps idle in 1815 was his leaving Serrurier's corps without orders for four days in Italy in 1797 when the rest of the army was marching pell-mell to meet an Austrian counter-offensive at Castiglione.

Bonaparte's intention for 16th June 1815 was to concentrate on destroying the Prussians under Blücher at Ligny. His plan was an old favourite – fix the enemy by frontal attacks while a second force marched round his flank and struck him in flank and rear. This was the same plan as against the Austrians in his very first battle, Montenotte, in 1796. His deployment of the army followed a familiar pattern as well – two separate wings, with a reserve which could join either wing, as necessary. The two wings would join on the battlefield. In the past these battlefield link-ups had not always succeeded – at Rivoli in 1797, at Marengo in 1800, at Eylau in 1807, Bonaparte had waited anxiously for important formations to turn up and save the battle. At Bautzen in 1813 Ney failed to fall upon the enemy's rear like an avalanche as intended, because of muddled orders. And on 16th June 1815 he failed again to fall upon the enemy's flank at Ligny according to Bonaparte's plan.

This is what was supposed to happen: Ney, with the French left wing, some 45,000 men, was to advance to the Quatre Bras crossroads, brushing aside what Bonaparte thought would be feeble opposition from such troops as Wellington would have been able thus far to get into the field. Then Ney was to swing east in order to take Blucher at Ligny in the flank, while Bonaparte was hammering Blücher with the French right wing, also some 45,000 men. Unfortunately Bonaparte's information and calculations were adrift. Instead of Blücher being there only in the strength of an army corps, perhaps 20,000 men, Blücher had got 84,000 on the ground – four fifths of the Prussian army. And Ney was blocked and beaten by Wellington at Quatre Bras in a hard-fought encounter battle, where Wellington's cool head and steady nerve saved the day as allied reinforcements came up piecemeal. Here was a potential Bonapartian self-inflicted wound indeed. At Ligny he was now struggling against Blücher with inferior numbers. He sent a pretty desperate signal to Ney telling him:

> At this moment the battle is very severe ... you are to manœuvre at once in such a manner as to envelop the enemy's right and fall with all your might on his rear ... the fate of France is in your hands.

But Ney himself by this time was also struggling against superior numbers, and there was no chance of his going to Bonaparte's rescue. The legendary Bonaparte ploy of uniting superior numbers on the battlefield in fact landed both him and Ney with inferior numbers.

I mentioned Lobau's 10,000 men left behind at Charleroi. There was of course another French corps of 20,000 men that did not fire a shot at either Quatre Bras or Ligny that day – D'Erlon's corps. Instead it spent the day marching to and fro between the two battlefields in obedience to contradictory orders. We cannot here argue about whose fault this was – Bonaparte's, Ney's, or an interfering *aide de camp* giving orders wrongly in Bonaparte's name. All I will say is that Bonaparte certainly failed to give any positive, clear orders to D'Erlon to stay with him at Ligny once he'd arrived, and let him slip away back to Quatre Bras in answer to Ney's orders. But more to the point, to have an army corps left out of the battle because of unclear orders was nothing new for Bonaparte. The most notable case is that of Souham, who marched between the main fronts at the battle of Leipzig in 1813 in obedience to varying instructions, and also never fired a shot.

In 1815 the want of D'Erlon's corps at Quatre Bras spelt failure for Ney, pitted against so superb a tactical leader as Wellington. At Ligny Bonaparte won, despite his inferior numbers, by sheer frontal bashing – partly thanks to the Prussian habit of deploying their troops on forward slopes to be mangled by French artillery fire. But it had been a close run, a needlessly close run, thing.

Now comes a series of Bonapartian self-inflicted wounds. The first was to believe without real evidence that Blücher was finished and making off

Napoleon in 1815, by Meissonier.

eastwards via Liège into Germany. In fact, as I've said, Blücher was retreating north on Wavre, to link up again with Wellington. Then, next morning, Bonaparte had second thoughts and despatched a force under Marshal Grouchy to find out if Blücher *had* separated from the English, or whether he might be in fact intending to re-unite with them to cover Brussels. He allotted to this reconnaissance 33,000 men and 96 guns – a third of his total strength. He also ordered Grouchy to pursue in a northeasterly direction, thus taking him outside Blücher's real line of retreat. A major dispersion of strength, and in the wrong direction.

As historians are well aware, poor old Grouchy was to get the blame from Bonaparte, and later from Bonaparte's historical partisans, for failing to turn up at Waterloo next day and save the battle. He's accused of showing want of independent judgement and initiative. Moreover, Marshal Soult, Bonaparte's chief of staff, also gets it in the neck for muddled and unclear orders to Grouchy – and indeed generally in the campaign. Everything, they say, would have been different if Berthier, Bonaparte's old chief of staff, had only been there. But would it? Certainly, orders issued through Berthier could be just as ambiguous as orders issued through Soult – could be despatched just as late, and arrive just as late. Jomini is a witness to this with regard to the 1807 and 1809 campaigns. Bonaparte was renowned for dictating instructions and letters; who can now say how far the phrasing of an order reflects Bonaparte himself, and how far a re-write by the staff officer? The truth is that Bonaparte was careless of detail, both in staffwork and logistics, and failed to ensure that key instructions were clearly drafted and promptly and safely despatched.

Failure to do this had got him into serious trouble before, when formations had turned up on the battlefields dangerously late or not at all – like Ney and Bernadotte at the battle of Eylau in 1807, or Ney at Bautzen in 1813. Now, in 1815, in a campaign of manœuvre with inferior numbers against an allied army of which one wing was commanded by Wellington, there was no margin whatsoever for slack or slow staff work, or ambiguous instructions.

Anyway, for the sake of clarity, let me follow through Grouchy's story. By the small hours of Waterloo day, Bonaparte had realised from reports that at least a Prussian corps had retreated north on Wavre. But he still failed to grasp the colossal danger to his right flank offered by the Prussian army. So what instructions did he now send Grouchy? Not to close on him at utmost speed; merely to advance northwest on Wavre, pushing the supposed Prussian 'corps' before him. The order was issued at 10 am and it reached Grouchy about 4 pm. By that time Grouchy had already been advancing towards Wavre for several hours. Back to Bonaparte again on Waterloo day, around 1 pm, about to launch his grand attack on Wellington, when he spotted Prussian troops some five miles off to the east moving towards him. Bonaparte now sent an urgent signal to Grouchy:

... do not lose an instant in drawing near and joining us, and crushing Bülow (the Prussian corps commander), whom you will catch in the very act....

This order reached Grouchy between 6 and 7 in the evening – far too late for Grouchy to march to Waterloo, and in any case he was by then tied down in a fierce action of his own with a Prussian corps. Grouchy had therefore been faithfully carrying out the instructions he *had* received, as Bonaparte expected his subordinates to do. He did not use his own initiative, and march to join Bonaparte as soon as he heard the distand sound of gunfire at Waterloo. Why should he? Bonaparte expressly demanded unquestioning obedience to orders, and disapproved of initiative.

Owing therefore to his own errors, Bonaparte found himself on the morning of 18th June with only two thirds of his army present, some 72,000 men, against Wellington's 68,000. Not an advertisement for Napoleonic principles of concentration at the decisive point. And of course, though Bonaparte did not yet know it, Blücher with 100,000 men lay some 8 miles to the east of his own flank and rear: a situation ripe with catastrophe.

For while Bonaparte was dividing and dispersing his own army, the allied commanders had been arranging to unite their own. Here I would stress that to talk of 'Wellington' and 'Blücher' and their armies as separate entities, or to think of Wellington fighting the battle of Waterloo until Blücher came to the rescue, is to have a false perspective on the campaign. Wellington and Blücher were commanding two wings of an allied army; their own personal mutual trust and collaboration ensured that; their agreed plan was to unite in defence of Brussels. In particular Wellington only stood on the Mont St Jean ridge because of Blücher's promise in the small hours of 18th June that he would unfailingly join him. In other words, it was the allies who had brought off the classic Napoleonic gambit – two wings which would unite on the battlefield: one wing to fix the enemy by frontal battle, and the other to take him in flank and rear.

The drawback lay in what Clausewitz calls 'friction' – the sheer difficulty of swift progress through narrow lanes turned to squelching mud by thunder-storms. It was the long delay before Blücher really got into the battle which exposed Wellington to several hours of single-handed fight against Bonaparte. But even so, the mere distant appearance of the Prussians compelled Bonaparte to detach 10,000 men to watch them, before he even launched his first attack on Wellington. So now Bonaparte would have to beat Wellington against the clock and with inferior numbers. All this was a consequence of mistakes on Bonaparte's side, and no corresponding strategic errors on the allied side, even though they had lost the battle of Ligny.

So now it all came down to whether Bonaparte could defeat Wellington in battle. Everything now depended on this; on the sheer fighting. But we must ask ourselves whether even a victory on the field could have long saved Bonaparte from the consequences of his strategic and political misjudgements. It is hard to imagine that commanders like Wellington and Blücher would accept the decision of one lost battle, like the Austrians at Marengo or the allies at Austerlitz – or indeed the Prussian monarchy itself in 1806. Harder still to believe that the coalition cemented in Vienna by Wellington and his colleagues would have come apart because of a lost battle in Belgium. Far more probable would have been a repetition of the patterns of 1813 and 1814, where Bonaparte's initial victories failed to bend his enemies' resolve to defeat him, and where he finally succumbed to superior numbers employed in a war of attrition. Indeed in 1815, after the escape from Elba, the allies were even more determined to rid Europe once and for all of this pest.

I don't want to repeat John Keegan's analysis of Wellington's conduct of the actual fighting at Waterloo, so I'm going to conclude my own remarks by briefly looking at the tactical self-inflicted wounds with which Bonaparte now followed his strategic ones.

There he was, around midday on 18th June 1815, having got himself into a plight where he was going to be squeezed between two enemy wings together outnumbering his own army by nearly two to one, unless he could defeat Wellington in pretty short order. In the past, he had several times been saved from the consequences of his own unsound strategy by the mistakes of his enemies – most of all the mistake of manœuvring to attack him, and so giving him an opening for one of his opportunistic strokes. This supplied much of the pattern of his early victories in Italy in 1796–7. It was true of his greatest victory, Austerlitz in 1805, in which the allies' attempt to turn his flank exposed them to a stunning counter-stroke which cut their army in two. Wellington proposed to make no such mistake at Waterloo – with an army of which less than half were British soldiers, and some contingents suspect material indeed, he was not going to risk what he called 'a false movement'. Bonaparte would have to break through a naturally strong position held in depth, more like Borodino or Aspern-Essling than Austerlitz, but against no ordinary general, rather a master of the tactical defensive.

Whether for the attacker or the defender, success in such a close tactical fight depended on the commander exercising firm and responsive control of his troops in the line. He must be able swiftly to sense the ebb and flow of battle; to seize without delay fleeting opportunities, and parry sudden dangers. It called, in a word, for personal leadership. This had always been Wellington's style; this was the way he was going to fight the battle of Waterloo, and in this fashion to maximise his chances.

Bonaparte, however, chose to command at second hand from behind the French line, at La Belle Alliance – some say Rossomme – sitting on a chair. He deputed Marshal Ney to exercise the front-line fighting leadership. Ney, ginger of hair and ginger of temperament, lacked the essential qualities for the role – no brains, no cool-headedness, no vision of the evolving shape of the battle. It was yet another of Bonaparte's self-inflicted wounds. Quite apart from the fact that Ney's tactical leadership could not begin to match Wellington's, the arrangement meant that Bonaparte himself had only a loose, sluggish and half-blind control over his army. Hence the French onslaught never had a theme; only disjointed attacks – disjointed both in time and in terms of the three arms of cavalry, artillery and infantry. In the case of Bonaparte's brother Jèrôme's attacks on the fortified farmhouse of Hougoumont, and later the death ride of the French cavalry round Wellington's infantry squares, Bonaparte had neither ordered them nor wanted them.

Thus Bonaparte even reduced his last, tactical chances by his own poor decisions. And when finally, more by luck than judgement, Ney at last got French troops on to the crest of the ridge in the middle of Wellington's line, and the opportunity was there for a moment of splitting the allied army in

Napoleon at Waterloo, looking suitably grim in defeat, but unrealistically close to the firing line.

two, the opportunity was lost because of Bonaparte's two-tier command system. Ney had to send a runner all the way back to Bonaparte to ask for reserves to smash through the breach. Bonaparte, out of touch with the front-line situation, and far more conscious of the danger to his flank from the Prussians, refused to release the Guard. Meantime Wellington, right on the spot, had seen and plugged the hole in his line; and the moment of supreme danger passed.

All the while, the Prussians had been pressing into Bonaparte's right flank and rear, so that the French line now formed a right-angle. I would say that Bonaparte now perpetrated the last of his self-inflicted wounds, and one which Wellington – and Blücher – exploited to bring about the total rout of the French army. The self-inflicted wound was this: by this time, about 7.30 pm, the French position was already hopeless and very dangerous, as I've pointed out. Instead of giving the order to retreat before it was too late – and using his last reserve, the eight battalions of the Guard, to cover the retreat – Bonaparte launched the Guard on a belated attack on Wellington's centre: the last of all the disconnected attacks of the day. When the Guard was repulsed, and the Duke waved his army down the slope, and the Prussians closed on the French rear, the consequence was the utter disintegration of the French army into a struggling mass of fugitives. Boney was done for – done for by his own errors and Wellington's clear and cool-headed generalship.

PART THREE

Wellington and Tactics

CHAPTER 7

The Myth of the Thin Red Line – Wellington's Tactics

The 'Thin Red Line' of the 93rd Highlanders at Balakclava. For artistic convenience the Russian cavalry is portrayed a quarter of a mile nearer to the highlanders than in fact it came.

I want to consider in this chapter just what it is that we mean by the commonplace phrase, 'the thin red line'. I think that if we can apply some precision in our analysis, we will reach a better understanding of the tactical methods which Wellington applied in his battles.

Actually the phrase is rather anachronistic if it is used in connection with Wellington's army, since it was first coined some forty years after Waterloo, as a misquotation from William Howard Russell's famous dispacth from the field of Balaclava in the Crimean War. Russell was describing a battalion of the 93rd Highlanders, and the exact phrase which he first used was 'a thin red *streak* tipped with a line of steel'.[1] Somehow this was taken up by his readers and transformed into a 'thin red line'. Russell stayed with this revision in his later descriptions of the battle. It makes a ringing phrase, and has the power to evoke an astonishing number of ideas and images. It was a phrase which encapsulated a patriotic myth which crops up time and time again in military literature.

As a phrase, the 'thin red line' means rather a lot more than might at first sight appear, and carries with it a number of unspoken assumptions. First of all, it contains a hint that the army is overstretched for the task it has to fulfil. At Balaclava there was only one paltry infantry battalion standing between an imposing mass of Russian cavalry and the main British supply dump and port. In other British battles and wars something similar seems to have recurred with considerable regularity. Whether it is Wellington operating in Spain with one small corps against several large French armies, or whether it is the Task Force recapturing the Falklands in 1982 from double its own number of Argentinians, the story is often the same. It is a thought which we can pick up again in Kipling's reference to what he called 'our far flung battle line'. A global Empire and an habitually small army have often left us overstretched.

Yet the second assumption is that our army will nevertheless be victorious. Although the redcoats fight outnumbered, they tend to win. At Balaclava the menacing Russian cavalry swerved away before it came to close range. A few distant vollies from the Highlanders were enough to turn it back, and hence remove the threat to our base. At Waterloo Wellington weathered the heaviest assaults which Napoleon himself could devise, and inflicted upon him the most rapid and complete defeat of his career. Of course the myth of the thin red line does not dwell on the numerous occasions when British forces have been defeated by inferior numbers: it is not concerned with the Saratogas or the Singapores. It is designed to show that 'British is best'.

Next we come to a rather more technical implication of the 'thin red line'. In this case it is one which Russell spelt out in his dispatch and which he appears to have taken from Sir Edward Creasy's description of Waterloo, which appeared in 1851. Creasy had talked of Picton's success at Waterloo with 'a thin two-deep line',[2] and Russell developed this idea to suggest that the British could habitually win battles with an exceptionally light tactical formation which foreigners would not dare to employ. Whereas other armies used heavy squares or columns to boost their morale, the British needed no such spurs to their courage. At Balaclava the 93rd scorned to form a square, which was of course the accepted formation against cavalry, thus making the point admirably. In Wellington's case it would be incorrect to suggest that the square against cavalry was scorned, for it was not; but we can at least find several impressive instances of British soldiers beating off cavalry before the square had been fully formed.[3]

In infantry fighting against other infantry, however, Creasy and Russell had a perfectly valid point, since it is true that the standard British drill from around 1800 onwards was to draw up each platoon or company in two ranks rather than the three which were favoured on the continent. We also find that the British tended to draw up their battalions in a line of platoons arranged side by side, and not in columns with one platoon behind the other. Technically speaking, therefore, there were at least two senses in which we can say that British infantry fought in thinner formations than other armies. Not only was each platoon formed thinner, but so was each battalion.

Once again we can find an even deeper implication in all this. The idea is that British troops, who alone can make these dangerously thin formations work, must be exceptionally cool, calm and collected. They must have a high degree of 'phlegm', and they must display all those qualities which were so much admired by our Victorian ancestors – the 'stiff upper lip'; the 'bulldog spirit'; or what we would today perhaps call 'the resolute approach'. Even though the Gatling's jammed and the colonel is dead, the stalwart British soldiers will continue to play the game. Waterloo was allegedly won on the playing fields of Eton and the 'Iron Duke' (himself a Tory prime minister in his day) was certainly a highly imperturbable character.

'Steadiness' is perhaps the best word to sum up all this. The thin red line can work only if the troops are steady. They must not 'bob' (or duck)

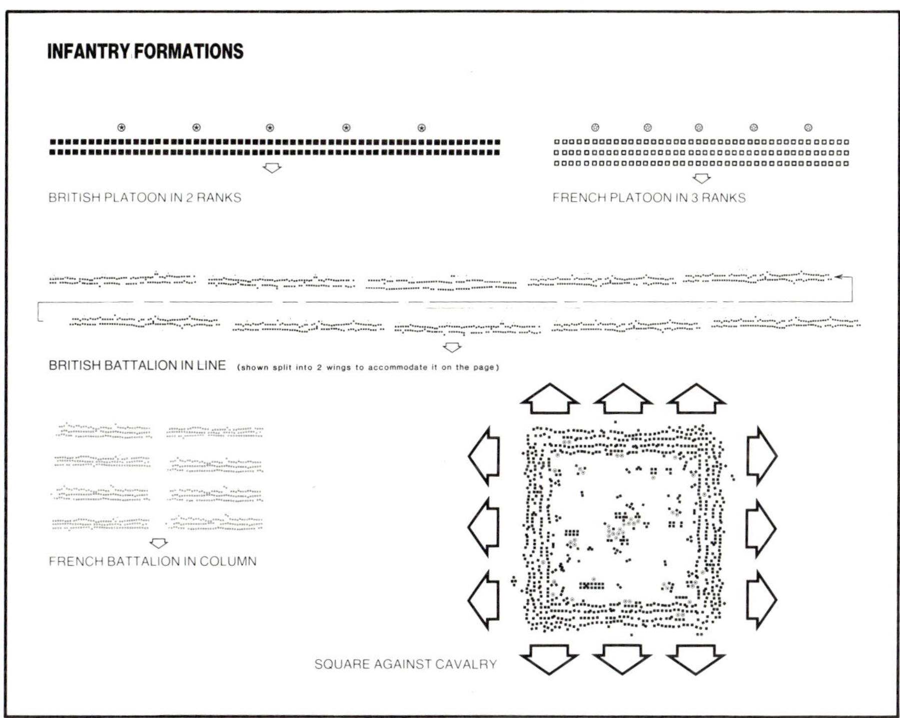

BELOW: A clash of column *versus* line in a defile.

too much when the enemy fires at them. They must not be too enthusiastic in the pursuit, nor too windy when the situation becomes serious. They must be capable of performing their drills and using their weapons regardless of the dangers or temptations they face. They must continue to do their duty without allowing either their emotions or their avarice to get the better of them. Wellington kept returning to these themes throughout his career. His favourite *bêtes noires* included troops who pressed their pursuit too far, no less than those who were diverted from their duty by either the fear of death or the love of plunder. Steadiness was the thing!

In clear contrast to all this was the equal and opposite assumption that all foreigners would prove to be somewhat lacking in steadiness. They would be excitable, mercurial and noisy. Thus at Balaclava, Russell was able to contrast the *sang froid* of the 93rd Highlanders with the behaviour of their allies the Turks. Some Turkish troops on the flank opened fire at the approaching Russian cavalry at a range of no less than 800 yards – well beyond the effective range of their muskets. Having performed this quite futile action the Turks then turned tail and fled the field. It makes a most striking parallel with the achievement of the Spanish at Talavera in 1809, who did very much the same thing on a grander scale. In both cases the British troops were deprived of their supporting forces very early in the action. Something similar happened in many of Wellington's other battles. At Busaco there was a Portuguese unit which ran away as a result of its own fire. At Waterloo there is a strong suspicion that some Dutch-Belgians did the same, although at least one Belgian historian has strenuously denied it.[4] Wellington's own attitude was certainly one of profound scepticism about his allies. His opinion of the Spanish was that 'They are really children in the art of war, and I cannot say that they do any thing as it ought to be done, with the exception of running away and assembling again in a state of nature'.[5]

If our allies were habitually considered windy and excitable, no less could be said of the enemy. Wellington in India saw no particular danger in attacking 60,000 Mahrattas at Assaye with 5,000 British troops. The enemy was bound to run away – and indeed he did so! In Denmark in 1807 Wellington even attacked 15,000 Danish militia with 5,000 British troops, and at Oporto two years later he attacked 11,000 French with a mere 600 British in the first echelon. When he was on the top of his form Wellington displayed an absolutely total contempt for all foreigners, and was prepared to take on any number of them. It was only a pity that he could not quite maintain his top form through his entire career. In the middle period of the Peninsular War for a couple of years he started to take an uncharacteristic interest in the combat odds – he started to count the French – and he was sometimes overawed by enemy numbers which were only slightly superior to his own. Michael Glover has outlined some of the reasons for this (see Chapter 2), but it does mark a break from Wellington's normal practice.

At Assaye and in other Indian battles it was the first determined onset which made the most telling impression upon the enemy.

There are many references in the literature which stress the contrast between British steadiness and French excitability and noisiness in Wellington's battles. An anonymous diarist in the British 71st regiment at the battle of Fuentes de Oñoro gives us the general message loud and clear. What he says is this:

> How different the duty of the French officers from ours. They, stimulating the men by their example, the men vociferating, each chaffing each until they appear in a fury, shouting, to the points of our bayonets. After the first huzza the British officers, restraining their men, still as death. 'Steady, lads, steady', is all you hear, and that in an undertone.[6]

Major Dawson Kelly of the 73rd regiment at Waterloo tells a similar story of a French attack which he received:

> Their advance was as usual with the French, very noisy and evidently reluctant, the Officers being in advance some yards cheering their men on. They however kept up a confused and running fire, which we did not reply to until they reached nearly on a level with us, when a well-directed volley put them into confusion which they did not appear to recover, but after a short interval of musketry on both sides, they turned about to a man and fled.[7]

A combat at close range between two columns of companies.

This was the British impression of the French in the attack. When it was their turn to defend, the French apparently demonstrated their lack of steadiness by opening fire too early. This fire would thus be wasted to no effect and the British would either be allowed to press home an assault, if desired, or to settle down in a protracted exchange of pot-shots, without excessive loss. Thus at Salamanca George Hennell's battalion was brought up to a French position, and he reported the action in the following terms:

We had express orders not to fire until ordered. Our regiment was well prepared to give them an excellent charge. Had they stayed still till we came up 20 yards further they might have given us a most destructive volley, but they rapidly fired a volley or two that passed mostly over our heads and they ran away.[8]

Again, at Vera in 1813 Hennell saw a similar transaction:

'The French, who delight in a long shot (the Spanish and they are well matched in this – famous ammunition wasters) began directly ... our men showed their heads. However the 9th moved regularly (I do not mean in a line) up the hill to within 30 yards of the top without firing and then, by way of breathing, gave a volley, loaded and advanced to the top, the support close behind them. The French did not attempt to defend it but moved to their left, not without music, in quick time.'[9]

Even in defeat the French maintained their noisiness, apparently!

Infantry acting as skirmishers would lurk in cover and act in pairs using individual initiative.

These passages also indicate that the British excelled in holding their fire right up to the last moment, thus helping them to maintain their own steadiness at the same time as they unnerved the enemy, who would be blazing away recklessly. At Balaclava the 93rd Highlanders actually did not hold their fire in this prescribed manner,[10] but fired their first volley at no less than 600 yards, which was beyond effective range. We cannot therefore say that this thin red line behaved in a way that was quite typical of Wellington's army, which may have possessed even greater steadiness in this particular respect.

A *single* volley at close range was all that Wellington's men usually delivered as they charged forward. In some cases they did not even need this. Thus private Wheeler in a skirmish at San Christoval in 1812 was told by his commander:

> 'My lads, you shall give them a taste of your steel directly.' We was soon within point blank distance of their line. Sir Thomas then gave the word double quick, in a moment thirty buglers was sounding the charge and off we dashed in double quick time with three cheers, and away went the enemy to the right about. We had now gained the ridge without discharging a single musket, our bugles sounded the 'halt' and 'fire'.[11]

This passage shows that the British could be quite as noisy in the assault as the French, although in this case the bugling and cheering were deliberate methods of command and control, or weapons against the enemy's *morale*. They were quite different in quality from the chattering, shouting and firing of a French unit in the assault.

At Talavera, John Aitchison reports that his unit charged the French 'when he was within 100 yards, and our fire was reserved until they were flying'.[12] Once again, we see a laudable British ability to avoid an indecisive firefight, but a willingness to close with the bayonet.

It is at our peril that we forget that Russell's thin red line was 'tipped with steel'. Its soldiers carried bayonets as well as muskets, and were no less adept in the bayonet charge than in the musket volley. It is here, however, that we come to the greatest misconception of all about the thin red line, so we must tread rather carefully.

The phrase 'the thin red line' suggests something splendidly immobile and stodgy. The British stand their ground and fire vollies when all around have fled. This is what happened at Balaclava and it is also, in a grander sense, what happened in many of Wellington's battles. The British often held a linear position against repeated French attacks. At Busaco they held the line of the great ridge. At Talavera they stood for two harrowing days

Cheering was an important part of battlefield technique. If well controlled and applied in mass it could be as effective as a volley in destroying enemy cohesion.

along the line of the Portina Brook. At Fuentes the line ran along the Dos Casas river and at Waterloo it ran along a farm track. In all these cases Wellington allowed the French to come and beat their heads against his position until they grew tired of the game. Nor was he usually able to pursue them with any energy when they withdrew from the contest.

A distinction we must make, however, concerns the level of action we are discussing. These linear positions of Wellington's were occupied by his whole army in each case. They were drawn up in a line at the 'grand tactical' or 'operational' level. What we usually mean by the 'thin red line', by contrast, is something much less grand. It is a line of only one or two battalions, acting at the *minor* tactical level. We should not therefore confuse these two ideas. It is true that Wellington often offered an immobile line at the grand tactical level, but it may not be true that his individual battalions were immobile within this general framework.

In fact they most emphatically were not. Wellington's battlefields were usually pulsating with activity, both laterally – as reserves were shifted from one point of danger to another – and from rear to front, as units were committed to the charge. Wellington was very much an attacking general in minor tactics, I believe, whatever may have been his approach to grand tactics.

The reasons for this mobility may perhaps be traced to Wellington's early experiences in India, where it was axiomatic among British officers that one always had to press on rapidly and knock the enemy for six before he had time to react or manœuvre. If you hesitated you were lost, since the enemy would then have a chance to regain his balance and take effective countermeasures. Wellington's battles and sieges in India were therefore notable for their rapid and daring assaults. Time after time the enemy had the initiative wrested from him at the point of the bayonet – the British bayonet.

In European warfare, by contrast, there was a certain reaction against this 'colonial' view. There was a distinct feeling that the 'big league' on the continent of Europe was a lot more demanding, since the enemy was liable to possess much more manœuverability and tactical responsiveness than the Indian princelings. When Dundas wrote his drill principles in 1788, therefore, he wanted British infantry units to be very careful when they exposed themselves to the dangers of the continental battlefield. In particular they were to fight primarily by musket vollies delivered from a thick red line, in three ranks. The lessons learned in the colonies were to be eschewed.

When Wellington returned from India to the European theatre in 1805, therefore, his military credentials were treated with suspicion in some official quarters. Cautious officers like the Duke of York, the commander in chief of the army, were anxious that precious British expeditionary forces should not be squandered in reckless offensives by 'sepoy generals'. Wellington's career suffered a certain set-back which he did not completely throw off until about 1811.[13]

In practice, Wellington did not let all this hold him back, and he soon stamped his mark upon every unit with which he came into contact. In the case of the Peninsular army there is plenty of evidence that he inspired his troops with the spirit of the bayonet[14] – and in defensive tactics no less than in the offensive. The best way to defeat a French attack seemed to consist of counter-charging it at the moment when it was most disorganised by its approach march, and at the peak of its psychological agitation. The thin red line would then surge forward in such a threatening and awesome manner that the enemy would instantly flee. Far from standing immobile and fighting by fire, indeed, it would operate in an exceptionally elastic and aggressive way.

An early portrayal of Busaco: the British charge downhill firing only a few shots as they come. The French break and run before contact.

There were three phases in Wellington's defensive tactics which were all equally important to the success of the whole, and all of which incorporated an element of manœuvre. These were firstly the preparation of the enemy during his approach; then the counter-attack by the main British line; and finally the exploitation and action by reserves. Let us look at these three in turn.

During the preparation phase the advancing French units were to be showered with lethal projectiles and disorganised as much as possible. Their natural apprehension and disorder were to be increased by long range weapons, which would also have the advantage of reassuring the British troops themselves. From over half a mile down to around three hundred yards the artillery would fire shrapnel or solid shot, and at closer range would switch to canister. Wellington usually distributed his batteries along his whole front so that an attack at any point would come up against at least one of them, while others fired into the flanks. Only at Vitoria was there a massed grand battery in the continental style, and that was largely determined by the narrowness of the ground.

Also essential to this preparatory phase was the action of light infantry. A swarm of sharpshooters would cover the front of the British positions and would blaze merrily away with rifles or muskets, harassing the French at the same time as they kept enemy skirmishers at bay. It was at this phase of the battle that any aimed shots would be fired, although because ranges would be long and targets would be small the proportion of hits would not be high. At Roliça rifleman Harris reports that he fired so fast that his barrel overheated,[15] and this can hardly have helped his accuracy. The French in the Peninsula certainly complained that their officer casualties tended to be excessively high, but whether that was due to a policy of selective assassination by British light infantry, or to the officers' own recklessness in rushing forward ahead of their men, I cannot say. There is evidence for both views, and officers are even known to have fought personal duels on the battlefield on occasion.[16] Our friends in green coats are often insistent that they managed to pick off French officers very accurately and systematically, but I personally retain a healthily open mind on this point.

Diagram from de Rottenberg's regulations for light infantry: the deployment of a skirmish line.

50 100 200 300
Fig. 1
Fig. 2
Fig. 3
THE ADVANCED GUARD OF A BATTALION

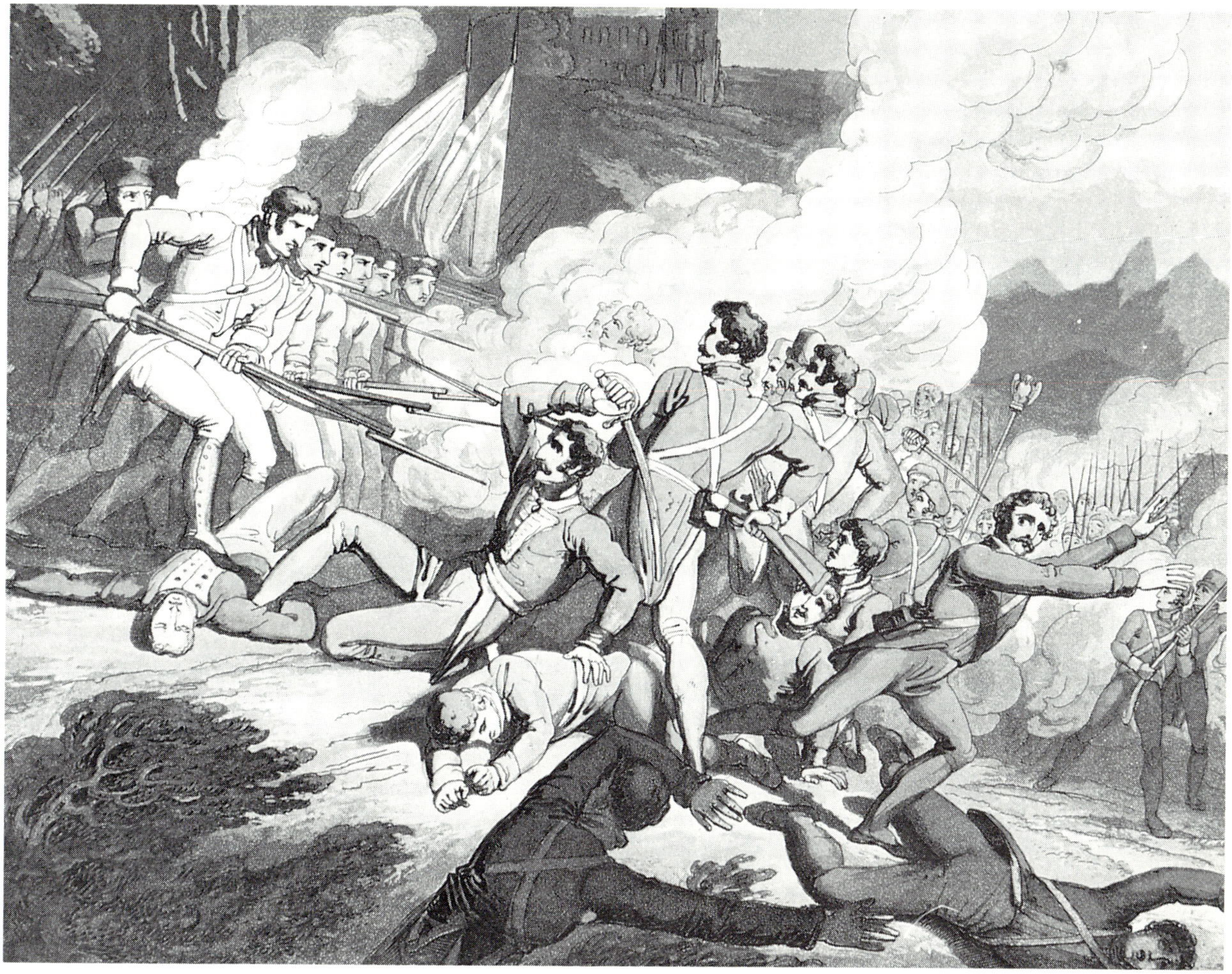

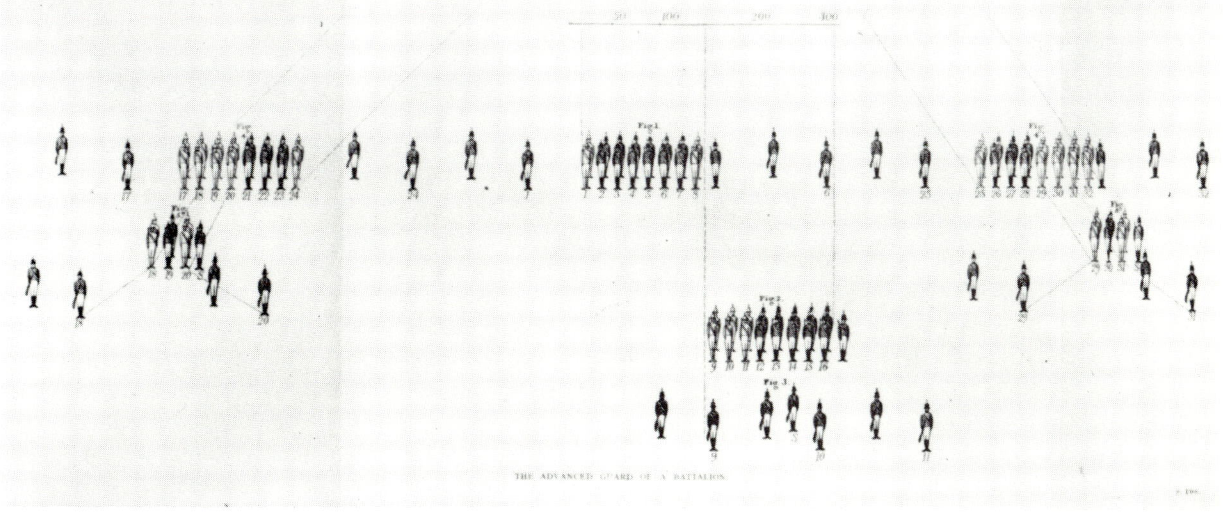

In Napoleonic fighting the point was not simply to defeat the enemy but also to plunder him.

The second phase of the battle would be the unmasking of the main infantry force from the covered positions in which it had been waiting. It might have been on a reverse slope behind the crest of a hill, or it might just have been lying down to protect itself from the enemy's fire. At the psychological moment, however, it would try to spring up and come forward with a single unaimed volley and a cheer. Because this force would be arrayed in a thin red line it would doubtless enjoy the advantages of overlapping the enemy's column. The attack could seem to engulf the French soldiers from all sides, thus overawing them all the more convincingly. I do not believe that the advantage of the line formation had much to do with the improved musketry which it offered, as has often been claimed, but it may be linked to the possibilities which it offered of making a flank attack.

When this counter-charge came near to the French it would almost always chase them away in confusion. The British would then race on in pursuit, doing as much bayoneting, firing and plundering as they could. The soldier on campaign would especially welcome any perks or home comforts which he could pick up from the fallen foe, quite apart from the symbolic satisfactions which can always be gained from a military trophy. This often led to disorder in the pursuit, and at Vimeiro one French force was pursued with enthusiasm for no less than two miles. This was hardly the action of a 'stolidly stodgy' or 'immobile' British line!

From Wellington's point of view it was the third phase of the battle which often posed the most difficult problems. If the thin red line did its

A later version of Busaco, showing almost indentical features to those of the top picture on page 157. The great strength of the terrain, at least, is here shown to greater effect.

work successfully, and did not pursue the defeated enemy too far, then all would be well. The line could be quickly re-formed and tactical balance regained. But if something went wrong in the second phase of combat there might be a serious problem in the third. In some of Wellington's polyglot armies the main line might not have been quite as steady as the highest British standards demanded, and on a number of occasions the French did actually succeed in penetrating it. In this case Wellington would be forced to plug the gap with a reserve.

At Fuentes the British right flank was forced back by a strong French attack, and Wellington had to change front with a half of his line. He afterwards admitted that the army came close to defeat on this occasion. It was only by a timely movement of reserves that the day was saved. Equally in the first battle on the Pyrenees his first line was posted at the passes of Maya and Roncesvalles, which were both forced by superior numbers of the enemy. They both had to retire to the reserve position around twenty miles to the rear, at Sorauren. Wellington was for a time hard pressed to gather sufficient reserves at this point, and was temporarily somewhat unbalanced. In the end he succeeded admirably, and in the event Sorauren was one of his finest actions – but the fact remains that it was a battle which was decided in the third tactical phase, rather than the second.

A runaway *success* by the 'thin red line' was often more serious than its partial defeat. At Talavera, for example, the British met the French onslaught with such a devastating counter-attack that the entire centre of the

British position ran away in the disorder of pursuit, and was chopped to pieces by the advancing French second echelon. This was a disastrous moment, and Wellington was hard put to it to bring up a small reserve and cover the rallying of his fugitives. As at Fuentes, he afterwards admitted that he had come within an ace of destruction.

All Wellington's defensive battles forced him to react to enemy moves, rather than to take the initiative himself from the start. He must often therefore have preferred to fight offensive battles, and his record of success in them is more clear cut. Assaye, Salamanca and Vitoria produced better overall results than any of the defensive battles except Waterloo ... and we do not need to be reminded what a near-run thing *that* was.

If we turn to Wellington's tactics in the attack we find very much the same pattern as we have seen for the defence. Fire preparation from skirmishers and artillery, if it was practicable, would be followed after a very short interval by a heady echelon assault by 'the thin red line', including the usual cheering and restraint on firing. Normally this would be enough to chase the French away, but if it failed then some shifting of reserves would be necessary to renew the pressure against that point. Attacks were easier to lay on than defences, however, since one had only to channel a succession of efforts against a single point, and the choice of the psychological moment to unleash the movement came earlier (and depended less upon the actions of the enemy) than in a defensive battle.

All in all Wellington's tactical system relied upon a succession of efforts in depth, whether in the defensive or in the attack. It was what in modern terminology might be called an 'elastic defence in depth' or an 'attack to the full depth of the enemy's position'. We can therefore contrast Wellington's very *deep* conception rather neatly with the popular stereotype of a *thin* red line. The latter was only one element in a much bigger picture, except perhaps at Balaclava itself, where the 93rd Highlanders stood alone with neither skirmishers in front of them nor reserves behind them.

A point which should perhaps also be stressed is that it was by no means only a *red* line which did the fighting. Green riflemen and blue gunners had an essential role to play in the preliminary phase, and multi-coloured cavalry sometimes took up the functions of a reserve to plug any gaps which appeared in the third phase. The cavalry was effective in this role at both Waterloo and on the left flank at Talavera, although in both cases it also threw itself into a most hopelessly typical confusion in the process.

The Peninsular War also saw Wellington making a sustained effort to train his blue or green-coated Portuguese allies, and later even the Spanish, up to a standard of efficiency comparable to that of the British. At the combat of San Marcial on the Bidassoa it was actually a thin blue line of Spaniards which beat off every French attack! At Waterloo, equally, a considerable proportion of the defence was conducted by black Brunswickers and blue Dutch-Belgians. Our patriotic pride in our scarlet 'lobsters' ought

This sketch of Fuentes de Oñoro was used by the Bank of England for the design of its five pound notes. Beyond the smoke of battle Wellington's infantry may be discerned launching one of their characteristic counter-attacks against a surprised French force.

therefore to be tempered by an understanding of the contribution which was made by these other groups.

Finally, our conclusion is that Wellington's battles were not really *linear* at all, at the level of minor tactics. They were fought by a dynamic system of movements which was a far cry from the unmoving *gravitas* which the Victorians liked to imagine. The bayonet, as colonel Lake told his men at the battle of Roliça, 'is the only weapon for a British soldier!'[17] The secret of that British soldier's success lay in his ability to hold his fire for longer than his French counterpart, and then to launch an astoundingly violent and unnerving counter-attack.

If the expression 'the thin red line' is taken to stand for British steadiness and 'phlegm' in battle, then it makes an accurate representation of Wellington's tactics. If it is made to stand for a passive and linear defence which relies upon firepower, however, then it is very misleading. One is tempted to adapt Voltaire's remarks about the Holy Roman Empire, and suggest that in this case the 'thin red line' was 'neither thin, nor red, nor a line'.

A Short Land Pattern Musket.

An India Pattern Musket, and socket bayonet.

India Pattern musket locks:
ABOVE: a lock with the earlier 'swan-necked' cock,
BELOW: a lock with the 'ring-necked' cock introduced in 1809.

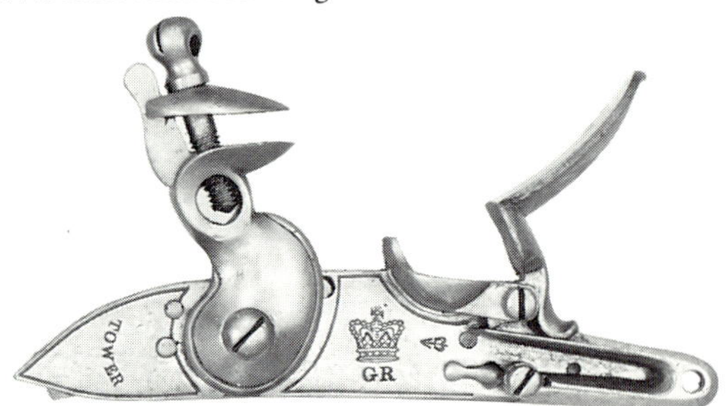

CHAPTER 8

The Weapons of Wellington's Army

GRAEME RIMER

Introduction

This chapter describes the major weapons used by the various component parts of Wellington's army throughout the Peninsular campaign and at Waterloo. To do this, it has been necessary to discuss independently the arms of the infantry, the cavalry, and the artillery. On the battlefield, however, the weapons of these divisions were constantly interacting with similar equipment of the enemy in any number of combinations, and their different functions cannot and should not therefore be considered as independent and isolated. As a study of the effects of contact in war of infantry with artillery, cavalry with infantry, and so on, the reader is strongly urged to consult the remarkable study of Waterloo by John Keegan.[1]

The Infantry

The sole weapon of the British infantry at the outbreak of war with France in 1793 was the flintlock musket, a cumbersome smooth-bored weapon which had changed little in design for over sixty years.

Often referred to as the 'Brown Bess', a name it never received officially and which is not recorded until the late eighteenth century, the proper title of the arm then in service was the Short Land Pattern Musket (see opposite page). This was simply a shortened version, approved in 1768, of the Long Land Pattern, which had been in service since the 1730s. It weighed about ten pounds, had a forty-two-inch barrel with a bore of 0.78 inches diameter, and fired a ball of a standard fourteen and a half to the pound. It was equipped with a socket bayonet with a triangular section blade about seventeen inches long, held in place on the muzzle by engaging a slot in the tubular socket over a rectangular iron lug which also acted as a rudimentary foresight. The robustly elegant stock extended to about four inches from the muzzle, and the barrel was attached to it by iron pins. The brass furniture was of a quite elaborate form, similar to that of the Long Land Pattern, and included four ramrod pipes to retain the iron ram-rod. The lock had the characteristic 'swan-necked' cock of the period.

In 1785 the Board of Ordnance, the body responsible for the supply of almost all military material at that time, employed the famous London gunmaker Henry Nock in experiments to design a suitable replacement for the ageing Short Land musket. In 1790, after a series of trials, an order was made to produce 'New Pattern Muskets, 13 ball to the pound, with steel rammers', and contracts for their manufacture were placed with Nock and another government contractor, Jonathan Hennem. Two types of musket were ordered, in fact, later to be termed, 'the Duke of Richmond's two Patterns' after the then Master-General of the Board of Ordnance.[2] In contrast to the Long and Short Land Pattern muskets, these were very plain, lacking the elegant form of the stock and having much simpler brass furniture. One type, the 'rammer to the butt' pattern (see below), had the

TOP: A Duke of Richmond's Musket, 'rammer to the butt' pattern, *c.* 1790. BOTTOM: A New Land Pattern Musket, *c.* 1802. Note the simpler form of the stock, similar to that of the Duke of Richmond musket, compared to those of the Short Land and India Pattern muskets on page 156.

unique feature that the channel for the ramrod was cut right through the stock, so that the ramrod rested on the inner facet of the butt-plate, the head lying at about the mid-point of the underside of the barrel. The intention was that the weight of the steel ramrod would be further back, making the musket rather handier. The second musket, the 'rammer to the muzzle' pattern and was of more conventional form. Both types of musket were fitted with Nock's remarkable 'screwless' lock which, once the mainspring was released, could be dismantled without tools. Only two screws were associated with the lock; one to operate the jaws of the cock, the other to secure the lock into its recess in the stock. This design was the most advanced flintlock ever fitted into a British military firearm, and we will see more instances of its application later in this chapter.

Despite a promising start, both Nock and Hennem found that the high standard of workmanship demanded by these muskets made them difficult to produce in quantity, and though the Board had ordered 10,000 of them, only a little under 3,500 were ever produced.

At the outbreak of war, therefore, the Board of Ordnance was in a desperate situation. No large-scale production of muskets had taken place during the experiments, the Short Land Pattern Musket was still in general service, and reserves of serviceable muskets were dreadfully low. In a bid to put a reasonable quantity of muskets into the hands of the army, the Board first tried purchasing foreign arms, but because of the very varied pattern and quality of these weapons, the Board was reluctant to issue them to regular troops.

In desperation, the Master-General asked the then Home Secretary, Henry Dundas, for help, and suggested to him that the Board should try to purchase as many as possible of the pattern of musket then being used by the infantry of the East India Company. Some 29,000 of these muskets were bought in 1793, but supply was still insufficient and the gunmakers then producing weapons for the East India Company were asked to send their pattern muskets, together with any trade pieces they had in stock, to the Board. The result was a great mass of cheap arms being sent to the Board's storehouses, but again wherever possible these were distributed to foreign troops in British service.

Finally, in 1797, the Board, under pressure because of the continued shortage of an adequate musket for general service, decided to adopt the 'India Pattern' musket, as the East India Company's musket became known, as the standard infantry arm (page 156).

The weapon was not as well finished as earlier muskets, but the demands of wartime production were for uniformity, speedy production, and reasonable reliability, rather than for excellence of manufacture. Standards of view and proof had to be lowered, and stock timber of less good quality had to be accepted, but this did not mean automatic acceptance for service, indeed many thousands of muskets were rejected by the Board's viewers as unserviceable.

The barrel of the India Pattern Musket was of usual musket bore (0.75 ins) but was of thirty-nine inches in length; three inches shorter than that of the Short Land Pattern. The stock was similar in form to that of the earlier musket, but the furniture was plainer, and the shorter barrel meant that only three ramrod pipes were necessary. The long triangular-section socket bayonet supplied for this musket differed little from that already in service.

The only change made to the India Pattern Musket during the Napoleonic wars was the replacement in 1809 of the elegant swan-necked cock of the flintlock with a less attractive but stronger and cheaper ring-necked one (see page 156). In the same year, a lighter version of the India Pattern was introduced for issue to sergeants. Of the same outline and with similar furniture this musket had a barrel thirty-seven inches long and of carbine bore (0.65 inches).

Evidence of the Board of Ordnance's dissatisfaction with the India Pattern arms is shown by the fact that with the Treaty of Amiens, the Board immediately set about producing a new musket. Called the New Land Pattern Musket (see page 158), this used some of the features of the Duke of Richmond's weapons; the simple stock, plainer furniture, and slides rather than pins to retain the barrel, and it had an improved lock with a flat lockplate. The barrel, however, was a return to that of forty-two inches, and the socket bayonet was held more firmly on the muzzle by the addition of a simple but effective spring catch. A version of this pattern was also approved for issue to light infantry. This had a thirty-nine-inch barrel equipped with a simple backsight, and a scroll grip on the trigger guard; features to assist the light infantry in the higher degree of marksmanship expected of them.

The resumption of war, however, stopped all production of New Land pattern arms as too few contractors had made the change over in manufacture, and once again the India Pattern was in full scale production. The light infantry musket of New Land type did go into production in 1811, but the total of 20,000 made at this time was probably all that were produced until after 1815. A gradual return to manufacturing the New Land Pattern arms was made by the Board of Ordnance with the end of hostilities in 1814, but this was soon countered at Napoleon's escape, and the India Pattern remained in mass production until his final defeat. It has been estimated that between 1793 and 1815 some three million India Pattern muskets were produced.

From the Infantry Clothing Regulations of 1802,[3] we have a good idea of the ammunition which the infantryman would have carried during the Peninsula and at Waterloo. 'Sixty Rounds of Ammunition to be carried by each Rank and File of the Guards and Regiments or Corps of Infantry when upon actual Service, twenty-four of which are to be in a Tin Case furnished on such occasions by the Board of Ordnance.... The remaining thirty-six Rounds are to be carried in a Pouch in which there is to be a double Box of Wood bored with this Number of Holes ... There is also to be attached to the Pouch and covered by the Flap, a small Leather Pocket for carrying Spare Flints, Turnscrews, etc. ...'

The 'Rounds' referred to were the standard musket cartridge of the period; a tubular roll of paper containing a musket ball and six drams of coarse gunpowder.

The loading sequence of the musket was this: Having fired his musket the infantryman would draw the cock of the flintlock back into its half-cock or safe position. He would then take a cartridge from his cartridge case and bite off the end of the paper wrapping where the powder was situated. He then poured a small amount of the powder into the pan of the lock and closed the combined steel (or 'frizzen') and pan cover. Standing the musket on its butt, he then poured the remainder of the powder down the barrel and placed the ball, still in the paper cartridge-wrapper, in the muzzle. Drawing the ramrod he then drove the ball down the barrel and rammed it firmly into the breech. Replacing the rammer in its channel in the stock, and bringing the cock to the fully cocked position, the infantryman was now ready to give fire.

The effectiveness of fire from the standard musket has been the subject of much work by contemporary and later writers. The fundamental fault

Detail of soldiers firing their muskets with bayonets fixed – an occasionally dangerous procedure when it came to ramming home the charge at the muzzle. The men in the centre is placing priming powder into the lock of his gun.

was that the ball was sometimes a good deal smaller than the bore of the musket in order that loading should be as rapid as possible, essential in volley-firing. This difference in size meant that when the musket was fired 'windage', the escape past the ball of the propellant gases from the exploding gunpowder, occurred, causing the ball to deviate at a slight angle from the direction in which the barrel was aimed as it left the muzzle. Speaking of the musket's accuracy, or lack of it, Colonel George Hanger, writing in 1814, had this to say:

> A soldier's musket, if not exceedingly ill-bored and very crooked as many are, will strike the figure of a man at 80 yards; it may even at a hundred; but a soldier *must be very unfortunate indeed* who shall be wounded by a *common musket* at 150 yards, PROVIDED HIS ANTAGONIST AIMS AT HIM; and, as to firing at a man 200 yards with a common musket, you may just as well fire at the moon and have the same hopes of hitting your object. I do maintain, and I will prove, whenever called on, that NO MAN WAS EVER KILLED, AT TWO HUNDRED YARDS, by a common soldier's musket, BY THE PERSON WHO AIMED AT HIM.[4]

Hans Busk, the father of the British volunteer movement in the 1850's and 60's, refers to this question in his support of the use of the rifle for all infantry,[5] saying that due to lack of skill in the use of the musket, and its inherent inaccuracy, Colonel Schlimmbach, an officer of the Prussian artillery, had observed 'during the wars of the First Napoleon, the indisputable fact, that on average, a man's own weight in lead ... was consumed for each individual placed hors de combat!' Readers are recommended, however, to a more recent and very fine study of this question by Major General Hughes.[6]

A close-range duel of musketry between two formed bodies. Such duels were rare, but they could be very deadly.

The field of fire from Arcangues church near Biarritz. In 1813 a small British garrison beat off all French attacks across this field, and forced supporting artillery to withdraw, by musketry alone.

By way of summary it must be said that the lot of the musket-bearing infantryman on the battlefield was an unhappy one. The musket, with its bayonet attached, weighed in the region of fourteen pounds, and on every firing produced a great quantity of dense white smoke from both its priming and main charge. This smoke, unless dispersed by the wind, had a tendency to form an acrid cloud around standing lines of infantry so thick that it could effectively blot out not only the activity on the rest of the battlefield, but daylight itself. After repeated firing the musket would become covered in grey soot from burnt priming powder, and the soldier's face would be blackened by gunpowder from biting the ends off cartridges. If he was unlucky he might also suffer 'infantryman's hand', by stabbing himself on the bayonet's sharp point while ramming the charge home; an occupational hazard in loading any muzzle-loading weapon with its bayonet fixed. All this was in addition to the hazards he faced from the enemy.

The Rifle

In the last years of the eighteenth century, after the beginning of the French Revolutionary wars, British troops encountered foreign levies and emigrant volunteer companies, many of whom were armed with short-barrelled, muzzle-loading Jäger rifles. Interest in this arm as an effective light infantry

Sir Ralph Abercromby, who particularly asked for riflemen to join his force in the West Indies, 1795.

weapon was such that it led the Board of Ordnance to consider the introduction of a pattern rifle for British service.

The Board had experimented with rifles earlier in the century, but these were usually breech loaders and had not been felt to be practical for service issue. The last of these, a screw-breech rifle designed by Captain Patrick Ferguson, actually saw very limited issue and active service during the American War of Independence, but it was not formally adopted, and after the war was largely forgotten.

It appears that as early as 1795 the greater accuracy of the rifle was already appreciated, and the lack of British troops so armed was highlighted when Sir Ralph Abercromby had to ask for Darmstadt riflemen during an expedition to the West Indies. In 1798 the Board of Ordnance purchased five thousand Prussian rifled muskets, (but these were found to be of poor quality and were issued only to foreign troops), and in the same year the War Office issued a translation of a German training manual for riflemen. Also in 1798 Jonathan Bellis, the Board's Master Furbisher, was asked for his opinion on a suitable rifle for British service.

From 1796 onwards, the Board was offered a variety of possible rifles by gunmakers from England and abroad. Finally, after a trial at Woolwich in 1800, a pattern of rifle by Ezekiel Baker,[7] gunmaker to the Prince of Wales,

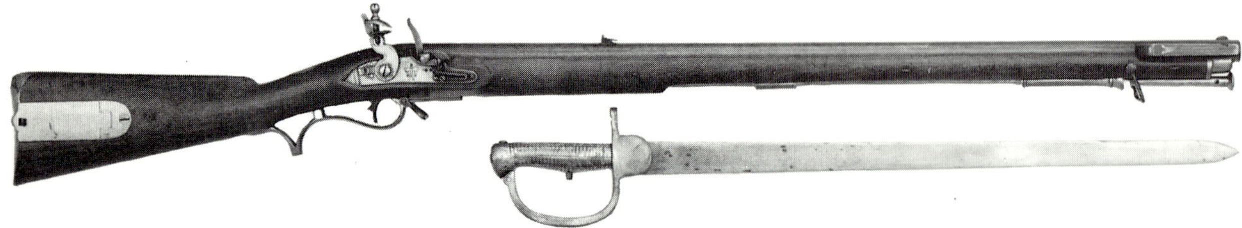

A Baker Rifle, with its distinctive sword bayonet. The rifle is a later example with a ring-necked cock.

was adopted for issue to an experimental rifle corps raised in that year under the command of Colonel Coote Manningham (in August that year to become the 95th Regiment or Rifle Brigade) (see above).

The design of the Baker rifle was strongly reminiscent of the German Jäger rifles. Its most important feature, its barrel, was thirty inches long, of round section, and its bore was rifled with seven rectangular grooves of equal width to the lands. The rate of twist of the rifling was one quarter of a turn in the length of the barrel. The stock extended to the muzzle and had a raised cheek-rest on the left side of the butt. The brass furniture included two of the most characteristic features of the Baker rifle; a scroll-type trigger guard giving a better grip for aiming, and a hinged patch-box cover set into the right side of the butt. Two large pipes retained the heavy iron ramrod, which was pierced with a hole beneath the head in order that a pin could be passed through to increase leverage when using the rod to withdraw a ball after a miss-fire. In earlier examples of the rifle the cock of the lock was swan-necked, but later the ring-necked type was used. The bayonet, also influenced by German designs, was in effect a short sword, with a straight single-edged blade twenty-three inches long and one and three quarter inches wide at the base. The cast brass hilt was equipped with a knucklebow. The bayonet had a slot in the hilt which fitted over a bar attached to the right side of the muzzle of the rifle.

The sights of this rifle were far superior to those of any musket, and consisted of a thick iron blade foresight brazed to the muzzle, while the backsight was a notched block set at 200 yards, with an attached folding leaf sight for 300 yards range.

The early Baker rifles were of musket bore but according to Baker, these were found by the troops to whom they were issued to be too heavy, thus the later rifles are of a bore giving twenty balls to the pound (0.625 inches). Baker also designed a rifled carbine for cavalry, which had a twenty-inch barrel and a ramrod attached to the muzzle by a swivelling link. Unfortunately we have practically no information on when or to whom this carbine might have been issued in the period before 1815. What we do know, however, is that the Baker infantry rifle remained fundamentally unchanged in its active service career through the Peninsula and Waterloo campaigns, indeed it saw service for a total of over forty years, the longest service life of any British military rifle.

The principle under which all rifles operate is that spiral grooves in the bore impart rapid spin on the projectile (in the case of the Baker a spherical lead ball) as it leaves the muzzle, the centrifugal force so generated assisting the ball in overcoming influences like wind pressure, or imperfections in the roundness of the ball's surface, and thus increasing accuracy. The Baker rifle, in common with most muzzle-loading rifles of the period, suffered from the disadvantage that for the rifling to have any effect the ball had to be a tight fit, and in a powder-fouled barrel loading was generally a slow business when compared to the loading of a musket. The procedure for loading was not unlike that of the musket with the exception that instead of using cartridges the rifleman had a powder flask and a pouch of separate lead balls. Having placed a measured charge of powder in the barrel the rifleman took a circular patch of greased cloth from the patchbox in the butt of his rifle, placed it over the muzzle, pressed a ball down into it, and drove the ball to the breech with the ramrod. Cartridges, it seems, were issued later to try to speed this rather awkward method, and balls of smaller diameter were sometimes issued if an emergency demanded rapid rather than accurate fire.

The Rifle Brigade was a light infantry regiment intended for skirmishing and sharp-shooting, but on many occasions proved that it could also act as line infantry. Probably the best-known actions in which the 95th played a central role were of course at Waterloo; at La Haye Sainte and the Sandpit. They earned a reputation as the best light troops in the British army, and one British soldier had this to say of them; 'Certainly I never saw such skirmishers as the 95th, now the Rifle Brigade. They could do the work much better and with infinitely less loss than any of our best light troops ... They were, in fact, as much superior to the French Voltigeurs as the latter were to our skirmishers in general.'

Riflemen skirmishing from cover during the retreat from Corunna.

The Infantry Officer

A Pattern 1796 Infantry Officer's Sword.

Until the middle years of the eighteenth century the British infantry officer had carried as his weapon, but also as a mark of his authority, a spontoon; a staff weapon some eight feet in length, with a leaf-shaped head surmounting a short cross-bar.[8] In organised and structured battlefield engagements such a weapon was probably manageable, but in the wooded terrain such as that encountered in North America and India in the 1770s it was a near-useless encumbrance. As a result we find infantry officers at that time discarding the spontoon and carrying only a sword. Finally the authorities recognised the trend, and in 1786 the Adjutant General ordered 'that the Spontoon be laid aside and that in lieu thereof the Battalion Officers are for the future to make use of swords ...' Infantry officers were to be provided with 'a strong, substantial, uniform sword, the blade of which is to be straight and made to cut and thrust, to be one inch at least broad at the shoulder and 32 inches in length'. The form of the hilt was not specified in the order, except that it should be 'if not of steel, to be either gilt or silver according to the colour of the buttons of the uniform ...' Today this hilt is generally recognised as the 'bead pattern', so called because of a group of usually five graduated beads or spheres forming a decorative feature of the 'stirrup' form knuckle-guard, and the side-ring. Ten years later the pattern of sword carried by the majority of infantry officers during the Napoleonic wars was introduced. This Pattern 1796 sword had a similar blade to that of the earlier pattern, but the gilt-brass hilt had two kidney-shaped shells, a curved knuckle-bow, an urn-shaped facetted pommel, and a wire-bound grip (see right). The blade was adequate for its intended purpose, but the hilt was rather easily damaged, and, even by early in the nineteenth century, officers wrote disparagingly of their sword. Despite this, however, it remained in service for some twenty-five years.

The officiers of Grenadier and Light Companies, as members of elite corps, tended to shun the 1796 pattern, and unofficially adopted light swords with curved blades. Again deciding to accept the inevitable, the authorities introduced official versions of these swords in 1803.[9]

The Cavalry

The principal cavalry weapon in British service during the Peninsula and at Waterloo was the sword, and the design of the two basic patterns carried by the light and heavy cavalry throughout this period, and the technique by which they were so successfully used, are directly attributable to one inspired cavalry officer, General John Gaspard Le Marchant.[10]

Born in 1766, the son of an ancient Guernsey family, Le Marchant had by 1793, after a difficult and often unpromising first few years, succeeded in obtaining a staff appointment as Brigade-Major in the Bays under General the Hon William Harcourt.

In 1793 the Bays were in France, forming part of a mixed brigade with Austrian and Prussian cavalry. Le Marchant had already become absorbed in the study of the equipment and cavalry practice of the foreign troops he had encountered, and in a combined attack on Cassel had the opportunity to see these in actual combat. He was especially impressed by the Austrians (though he thought them 'terribly cruel' in their treatment of defeated troops), and wrote that he hoped that he would be able in time to train the troops under his command in the manner of the Austrian cavalry, 'who at present are superior to us as we are to the trained bands in the city'.[11]

The light and heavy cavalry swords in British service at the time were basically of patterns introduced in 1788.[12] Both types were unsatisfactory; particularly that for heavy cavalry, whose long straight heavy blade and large basket guard gave poor balance, leading to many instances in combat of the British cavalry trooper injuring himself, or his unfortunate horse, with his own sword.

On returning home in 1794 Le Marchant set about redesigning the British cavalry sword, and found amongst the many Birmingham and Sheffield sword-cutlers whom he visited, the maker Henry Osborn to help him in his work. Early in 1796 Le Marchant submitted his findings to the Commander-in-Chief, the Duke of York, in the form of 'A plan for constructing and mounting in a different manner the swords of the Cavalry'. These results were submitted to the Board of General Officers and were formally accepted for implementation on the 27th June.

The Pattern 1796 Light Cavalry sword is probably the best known of all British cavalry swords, and at the time of its acceptance was a radical departure from earlier designs (see page 168). The strongly curved blade, reminiscent of the Indian *tulwar* and Turkish *kilij*, was about thirty-three inches long (measured in a straight line from hilt to point), by one and a half inches wide, and made this sword a fearsome weapon. (So much so that a French general commander is reported to have wished it banned from the battlefield after witnessing its effectiveness in the Peninsula.) The simple iron 'stirrup' hilt, with a leather-bound grip protected by an iron back-piece, afforded little protection for the hand, although this was not apparently felt a great disadvantage since swords of this pattern are recorded in service with volunteer regiments as late as the 1860's. The scabbard was a plain iron one, hung from a waist-belt.

The Pattern 1796 Heavy Cavalry sword (see page 168) was, in stark contrast to that for the light cavalry, an ineffective weapon. It was in fact a direct copy of the Austrian Model 1775 'Pallasche für Kürassiere, Dragoner und Chevauxlegers', and it is possibly the Austrian connection which explains Le Marchant's choice of such a weapon. It had a straight single-edged blade thirty-five inches long and one and a half inches wide, and with a hatchet point. The hilt consisted of a heavy sheet iron disc pierced with oval and D-shaped holes, with a flat knuckle-bow projecting from a point

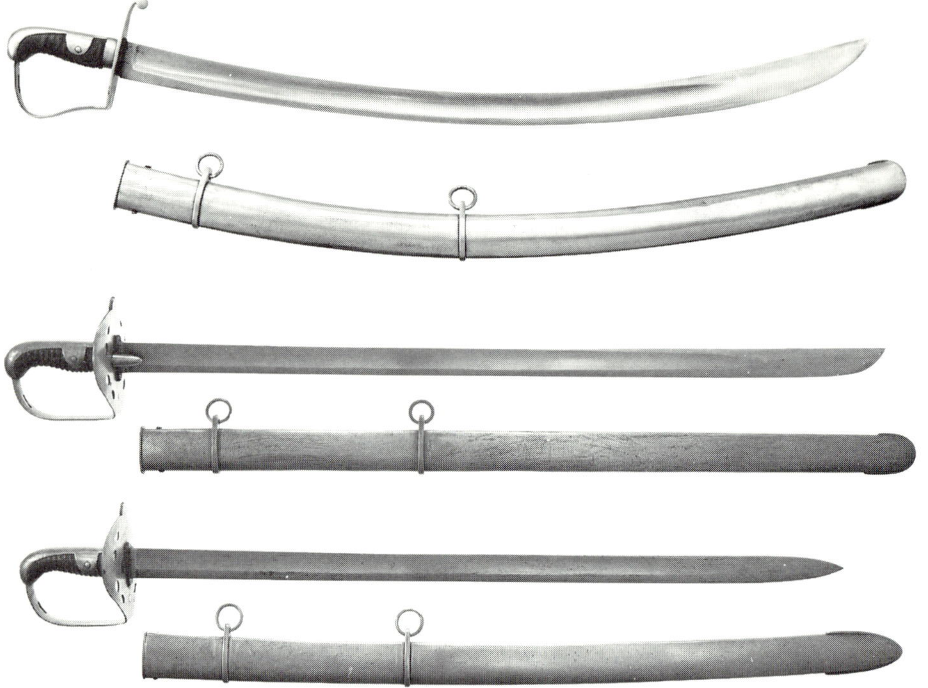

Cavalry Trooper's Swords:

A Pattern 1796 Light Cavalry Sword.

A Pattern 1796 Heavy Cavalry Sword.

A Pattern 1796 Heavy Cavalry Sword with a blade modified to a spear point.

in line with the edge of the blade. The grip was not unlike that of the light cavalry sword; a leather-covered wooden core fitted with a large iron back-piece. The plain scabbard, again like that of the light cavalry sword, was of iron.

The great weakness of this sword was the blade, which being straight was unsuitable for effective slashing, and whose hatchet point was hopeless for thrusting. An interesting comment on the effectiveness of this blade, which has been quoted by Mr Robson in his fine work on British military swords,[13] is one from Captain Bragge of the 3rd Dragoons, writing of a cavalry action at Bienvenida, in the Peninsula, in April 1812: 'It is worthy of remark that scarcely one Frenchman died of his wounds though dreadfully chopped, whereas twelve English Dragoons were killed on the spot and others dangerously wounded by thrusts. If our men had used their swords so, three times the number of French would have been killed.'

It is clear that it was this inability to make an effective thrust with the standard blade which led to an order to the heavy cavalry shortly before Waterloo that they were to 'grind the backs of their swords', meaning that they were to create a spear point in place of the hatchet. A sword so altered, and with a scabbard modified to match, is in the Armouries of the Tower of London (No IX – 251) (see above).

The large disc of the hilt was also a nuisance, the inner edge chafing the wearer when the sword was being carried, thus this part of the hilt is often found on surviving examples to have been removed. So frequently does this occur that it was almost certainly on officially sanctioned modification.

Despite all the shortcomings of this sword, however, it remained in service until it and the light cavalry sword were replaced by new patterns in 1821.

The hilt of a Pattern 1796 Heavy Cavalry Officer's Undress Sword.

The swords of 1796 pattern carried by officers, though privately purchased, varied little in form from the issue weapons of the troopers. The light cavalry officer's sword differed only in having various minor features changed in its hilt design, and having a fishskin-covered grip. The blade was often etched, blued and gilt. The blade of the heavy cavalry officer's undress sword was of the same form as that of the troopers, though often decorated, but the basket-guard of the hilt was of a robustly elegant curved form pierced and engraved with eight scrolls in the dish, and with a characteristic 'ladder' arrangement of holes in the broad knuckle-bow (see below left). A heavy cavalry officer's dress sword had also been introduced in 1796, but this is not really relevant to the present chapter. One other sword, however, though not an officially approved one, was worn by some officers during the Napoleonic wars. After the Egyptian campaign in 1801 it became fashionable among general officers, and officers of light dragoons, to wear a light curved-bladed sword with a simple hilt of so-called 'mameluke' type, inspired by the design of the native swords officers had seen in Egypt. Swords of this form finally reached pattern status for the first time in 1822 and as full dress swords are still worn today.

Sword-play between cavalry. In this case they are all slashing rather than lunging – a technique requiring less training but causing fewer serious casualties.

While Le Marchant had been devising the most suitable swords for the cavalry he had also been spending a great deal of time and energy in working out a series of cavalry exercises, which would, he hoped, bring a standard practice throughout the service, in place of the very variable quality of training previously given to cavalry troopers. Having devised these exercises he began teaching them at various centres around the country, and finally, in 1796, the War Office published (anonymously) his work as 'Rules and Regulations for the Sword Exercise of the Cavalry', with an order that it was 'to be observed and practised by the Cavalry Corps in General'.

Le Marchant's exertions in the training of officers were to lead him a few years later to found the Royal Military Academy at Sandhurst, but sadly Wellington was to lose this most remarkable cavalry officer to a French musket ball at Salamanca in 1812.

It is perhaps appropriate, before moving on from the edged weapons of the cavalry, to mention that at no time during the Peninsula or at Waterloo were lances used by British cavalry. The first encounter of British cavalry with lancers was in September 1811, near Ciudad Rodrigo. The lancers were Polish, and Tomkinson, an officer of the 16th Light Dragoons, wrote of the engagement, 'They (the lancers) looked well and formidable before they were closed to by our men, and then their lances were an encumbrance.'[14]

The lance, with its greater length, had obvious advantages in some circumstances, but on the occasions when lancer troop and sword-equipped cavalry encountered each other on the battlefield a resolute swordsman was generally felt to be at no great disadvantage. If he successfully evaded the point of the lance, a by no means uncommon occurrence in a charge, he was in a much stronger position than was the lancer who was hampered by his suddenly almost useless weapon.[15]

Some British cavalry officers had obviously been impressed by what they had seen of enemy lancers during the Napoleonic wars, but it was not until after Waterloo that any regiments in British service were converted to lancers.

Firearms of the Cavalry

Although, as we have seen, the principal weapon of the British cavalry was the sword, both light and heavy cavalry also carried firearms. Like the patterns of swords they carried, the carbines and pistols issued remained fundamentally unchanged throughout the Peninsula and Waterloo campaigns.

The standard carbine for light cavalry throughout the period was one which had been named after the officer commanding the 15th or King's Own Royal Light Dragoons, General George Augustus Eliott, and which had been approved by the King in 1773 for adoption into the service (see next page).

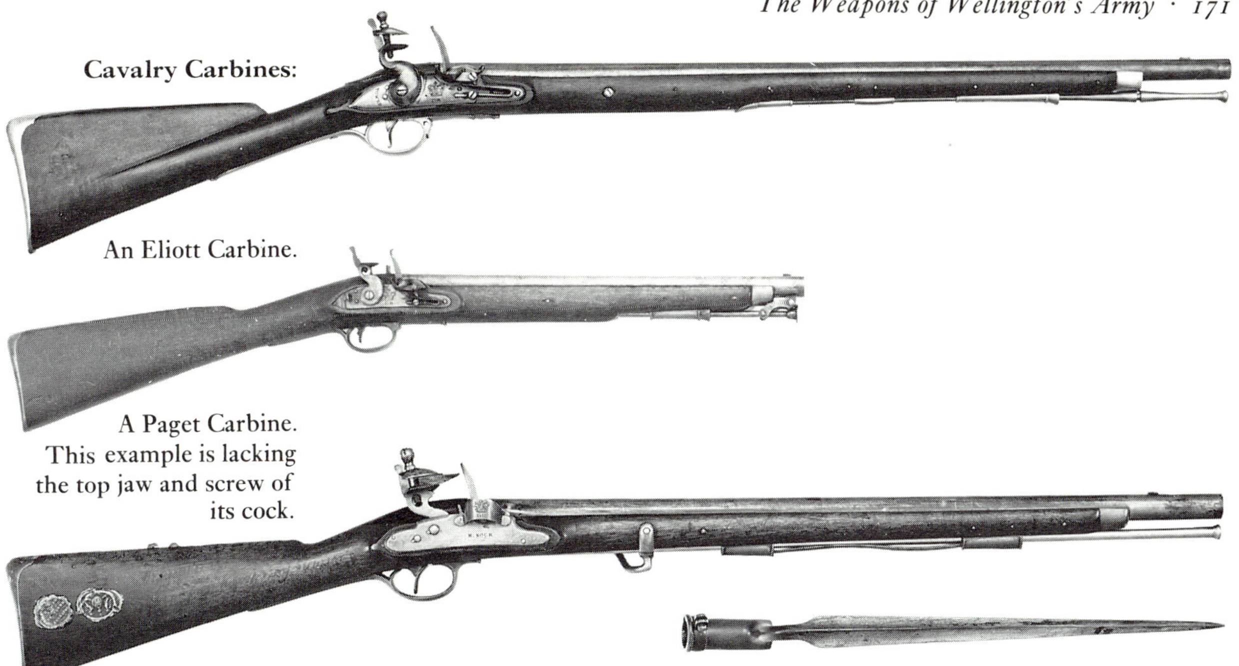

Cavalry Carbines:

An Eliott Carbine.

A Paget Carbine. This example is lacking the top jaw and screw of its cock.

A Pattern 1796 Heavy Cavalry Carbine. This is a sealed pattern example approved by the Adjutant-General, and is fitted with Nock's 'screwless' lock. As originally supplied to heavy dragoons this example is equipped with a socket bayonet.

The Eliott carbine was of course a flintlock arm, with a smooth-bored barrel twenty-eight inches long with a calibre of 0.66 inches. The stock, its brass furniture, and the overall manner of construction, were strongly reminiscent of the India Pattern musket described in the Infantry section of this chapter, except that screwed to the left side of the stock, extending forward from the rear side-nail (lock-screw), was a stout iron sling-bar with a loose iron ring attached, which allowed the trooper to hang the carbine from a large hook attached to a broad cross-belt. The unique constructional feature of the Eliott carbine, however, was that the iron ramrod was cut with a groove around a swelling a few inches below the head. When, after loading, the ramrod was pushed fully home into its channel in the stock this groove engaged with a lip on the underside of the brass fore-end cap, and very effectively prevented the ramrod from being shaken or jolted out by the activity of riding, or when the carbine was fired. To lose the ramrod of any muzzle-loading arm meant that the weapon was suddenly useless. To infantry troops recovery of a dropped ramrod was feasible, but to cavalry in action such a recovery would be practically impossible. This simple feature of the Eliott carbine doubtless prevented the loss of many a ramrod.

It has been suggested by past writers on the subject of British arms of the Napoleonic wars that the Paget carbine (see above) had been the light cavalry's mainstay from the Peninsula onwards. Named after General Henry Paget, this carbine had a barrel of the same bore as the Eliott, but of a much handier sixteen inches in length. The stock was of simple design in keeping with New Land Pattern arms, the barrel retained by slides rather than by pins, and perhaps most importantly the ramrod was permanently attached by a swivelling link beneath the muzzle.

It has been maintained until recently that the Paget carbine was introduced in about 1808, and indeed orders for its manufacture do appear at that time. Recent research has shown, however, that, possibly due to a reluctance to begin manufacture of a new pattern arm in wartime, the production of the Paget did not begin until late in 1812, and it is by no means certain, therefore, exactly how many carbines of this type had reached light cavalry regiments by the time of Waterloo.[16]

In keeping with their role as shock troops the carbine issued to the heavy cavalry was a rather more substantial weapon than were the light cavalry's Eliott and Paget carbines. Called the Pattern 1796 Heavy Dragoon (or Harcourt's) carbine, it had begun life in 1794, when a batch of newly designed carbines were supplied by Henry Nock to General William Harcourt's regiment, the 16th or Queen's Light Dragoons (see page 171).

The design, hardly surprisingly given the supplier, followed that of the Duke of Richmond's series of weapons, with simple stock form and furniture, and the original examples were fitted with Nock's highly successful but rather costly screwless lock. The barrel was twenty-eight inches in length, and of musket bore (0.76 inches), as part of an attempt to use a single size of ammunition throughout the service. To overcome the ever-present threat of a lost ramrod a long strip of spring steel was rivetted between the two brass ramrod pipes in order that its inward curve should hold the heavy iron ramrod firmly in place. The carbine was fitted with a

Hussar on patrol holding his carbine ready to sound the alarm. When not in use it would hang from the crossbelt over his left shoulder.

sling bar so that it could be hung from a cross-belt in the same way as that for the light cavalry.

At the time of this carbine's arrival with Harcourt's regiment the Board of Ordnance was seeking to standardise its cavalry firearms, and in 1796 its committee finally chose this design for adoption for all heavy cavalry. For a time little changed in its design, but in about 1798, when contracts for large-scale manufacture were being placed with suppliers in London and Birmingham, the screwless lock was dropped, on the grounds that it was too costly to manufacture and required greater skill on the part of the lock-maker than did the standard government flintlock. Production of the screwless lock had proceeded for some time, however, and it is almost certainly the case that Pattern 1796 heavy cavalry carbines with locks of both types saw service in the Peninsula and at Waterloo.

Despite sustained and often heartfelt pleas by cavalry against the need to carry a pistol, because of its near uselessness as a weapon on the battlefield, both light and heavy cavalry were issued with pistols throughout the period with which we are concerned. Both types of cavalry seem to have been provided with one pistol for each trooper, to be carried in a holster mounted on the saddle.

The design of the pistol for light cavalry had been established in the middle years of the eighteenth century, and had changed little by Waterloo (see below). It had a nine-inch barrel of carbine bore, a lock with a curved

Cavalry Pistols:

A Pattern 1796 Heavy Cavalry Pistol. This is a later example fitted with a ramrod and a conventional government pattern lock.

A Light Cavalry Pistol.

A New Land Pattern Light Cavalry Pistol.

lockplate and swan-necked cock, a plain stock with simple brass trigger guard and butt-cap, and a brass-tipped wooden ramrod held by a single brass pipe.

The heavy cavalry's pistol was another Henry Nock design, again of a pattern introduced in 1796, and was radically different in design from the light cavalry pistol (see page 173): Although the barrel was the same length as that of the light cavalry pistol it was of musket bore, and was fitted in a heavy stock devoid of any furniture except a small brass trigger guard, even lacking a ramrod, since this was intended to be carried separately in a holder attached to the holster on the saddle. This last feature was apparently not a popular one, however, as records and surviving examples show that pistols were later modified to take a ramrod in the usual way. The locks for these pistols were initially of Nock's screwless design, but contracts were later issued for pistols of this pattern to be made with the conventional government flintlock.

We know very little about the pistol issued to Household Cavalry regiments. A new pattern had been introduced in the first years of the nineteenth century as part of the New Land series of arms (see page 173). Similar in outline and bore to the light cavalry pistol, it had an improved lock and a ramrod which was attached by a swivel. A notable weakness in the design was the absence of a ramrod pipe, which meant that, if hurriedly used, the ramrod, held at an angle to its channel by swivel-link, tended to split the stock at the point of entry of the ramrod. Many surviving examples of this type of pistol are fitted with metal plates to reinforce this area, apparently having been repaired in this way by regimental armourers, as two of these plates are rarely the same. As with most New Land Pattern arms in the period 1809 to 1815, we simply do not know when or how many of these pistols were issued.

We have already looked, to some extent, at the effectiveness in battle of the British cavalry sword, but assessing the weapons effectiveness of cavalry firearms of the period is much more difficult. We have also discussed the loading procedure involved in the use of the musket, thus the problems facing the cavalryman attempting the same sequence of priming the pan of his carbine, pouring the rest of the powder from his cartridge down the barrel, ramming, replacing his ramrod then giving aim and firing, all while seated on a possibly agitated or frightened horse, can easily be imagined. The trooper would have also had problems with ammunition. Even if both firearms he carried were of the same bore size he would have to remember to lose some powder from his carbine cartridge before loading his pistol if he was not to have it blown from his hand. The problems outlined above make it impossible to estimate any rate of fire which might have been expected from cavalry firearms, they could only have been used as and when the situation permitted it.

The tactics used by British cavalry during the Peninsular and Waterloo campaigns are really too complex to be dealt with adequately here,[17] but it is true to say that the traditional roles of light cavalry as the highly mobile skirmishers, and the heavy cavalry as the main shock force, were largely adhered to.

The instances of success of one side or the other when cavalry met cavalry are as varied as they are numerous, a point which has been brilliantly examined by John Keegan in his analysis of the presence of single combat on the battlefield. It seems to have depended largely upon the willingness of both sides to engage, since when charging sword in hand it was of course impossible for two groups of troopers to get within effective range of one another if the horses they rode were packed tightly together.

Against well-drilled and steady infantry which was formed into square the cavalry, with the exception of one remarkable recorded instance, could make no real impression. The instance was in the Peninsula, in 1812, at Garcia Hernandez, when a trooper and horse of Bock's Dragoons of the King's German Legion, who were charging a solid French square, were simultaneously shot dead but crashed on into the solid wall of bayonets when no live pair would have done. Thus breached the square was quickly overrun by the Dragoons.[18] This incident illustrates the point very well that when confronted by infantry cavalry was often ineffective unless supported by artillery, the horse in this case acting in the manner of a great cannonball.

A cavalry attack, with curved sabres, against an infantry square. Such an attack would not normally succeed in coming to grips at such close range.

The Artillery

European field artillery of the eighteenth century was fundamentally little different from that in use from the middle years of the fifteenth century. It still consisted of a heavy smooth-bored barrel, usually of cast bronze, mounted on a two-wheeled carriage, and loaded at the muzzle with powder and ball.

Several important improvements to this simple device, however, made during the last years of the eighteenth century, had by the beginning of the Peninsular campaign brought smooth-bore artillery to a point of perfection which was to remain until it was eclipsed by the advent of rifled ordnance some fifty years later.

All field guns had to be aimed by traversing the heavy trail or rear of the carriage to one side or the other, and by elevating or depressing the barrel by the use of handspikes (long wooden levers), and fixing the barrel at the required angle by placing a large wooden wedge or 'quoin' beneath the breech. Fired from a horizontal barrel on level ground a solid iron ball would fly for perhaps 400 yards before hitting the earth, thus no elevation of the barrel was required. For greater ranges, however, it was of course necessary to overcome the effects of gravity on the projectile by angling the barrel upwards. Until about 1700 the necessary degree of elevation was achieved by using a 'quadrant'; a graduated scale and plumb line attached to a staff laid inside the bore of the cannon. An improvement in this situation was the marking of lines on the side of the breech, which, when used with a foresight on the side of the muzzle, gave quarter-degrees of elevation, but the most significant advance was the invention of the 'tangent sight' in the last years of the century. This consisted of a graduated post which could be set into a hole in the breech of the cannon, and which was fitted with a movable cross-bar cut with a notch to act as a backsight. Moving this cross-bar up or down, according to the range marked on the scale, then raising or lowering the breech until the target could be seen over the foresight, eliminated much of the earlier guesswork and inaccuracy.

The second major improvement was the replacement by the middle of the century of the laborious and inaccurate handspike-and-quoin system of elevation by a vertical elevating screw. The upper end of this heavy iron screw was firmly attached to the cascable (the large knob at the rear of the barrel), while the thread passed downwards through a block in the trail of the carriage. Elevation was controlled by a threaded handwheel.

In addition to these improvements British light field artillery benefitted from one further important development during the years before the Peninsular campaigns: Until this time gun carriages throughout Europe had consisted of two heavy parallel baulks of timber known as 'brackets', which were set edgeways and braced by 'transoms' (stout blocks of timber) passing between them. Beneath the forward ends of the brackets was the heavy axle, and above this the upper edges of the brackets were notched to receive the 'trunnions', the supporting lugs on each side of the barrel. The edges of each bracket were reinforced by iron bands, and numerous iron fittings added to the already considerable weight. The problems involved in transporting and accurately firing artillery on such cumbersome carriages prompted various European countries to seek methods of building lighter pieces. In England this, the last significant improvement to smooth-bore ordance, was the introduction by General Sir William Congreve in 1792 of a block-trail carriage. This had a single baulk of timber in place of the earlier two, and was a great deal lighter. Not only could a gun now be traversed by the commander of the gun (where before this required two of the guns detachment each with a handspike and operating under instruction from the commander), but the gun could be drawn by fewer horses.

By the early nineteenth century the sizes of guns had become standardized. In England, as in several other European countries, though not in France, these were 3, 6, 12, and 24 pounder (pdr) guns, their designation being taken from having bores the diameter of an iron ball of that weight. From experience in the later years of the eighteenth century of smaller colonial wars, where light artillery was found the most useful, the brass 6 pdr became the standard British general-purpose gun. A gun of this type had a barrel five and a half feet long, with a bore diameter of 3.7 inches, and weighing about six and a quarter hundredweight. At the time of the Napoleonic wars such a piece would have required a team of six or eight horses to draw it.

From early in the Peninsular campaign, however, the 6 pdr was being outclassed by the French 8 pdr guns. In response to this a 9 pdr gun, a size which had been dropped from British service in the middle years of the eighteenth century, was reintroduced, and was to prove very successful, replacing by Waterloo about half of the 6 pdrs then in service.

The standard British light gun of the Napoleonic wars; the light 6 pdr. This example, in the Museum of Artillery in the Rotunda, Woolwich, has a barrel which was cast in 1796 by F. Kinman, and the Congreve pattern carriage is one of the very few surviving original examples. The wheels, of the correct type, were replaced in 1862.

The ammunition available for guns in British service was of four types:

Round Shot: Simply a solid cast-iron ball, this was by far the most common projectile for artillery, and comprised perhaps seventy or eighty per cent of the total quantity of ammunition in the supply train during the period of the Peninsular campaign. In larger calibres (18 and 24 pdrs) round shot could be used for the breaching of fortification, but in lighter guns its purpose was as a general-purpose projectile for use against any opposing force, be it infantry, cavalry or artillery.

When used against a massed target round shot could produce frightful results. Fired from a gun at point blank range (i.e. with no elevation) the shot would fly for perhaps three or four hundred yards without rising above the height of a man, before striking the ground, when it would bounce or ricochet for perhaps as great a distance again. Contemporary and later artillerists[19] estimated that a single round shot could be expected to kill on average three men, but in close formation the casualty rate was often higher; at Waterloo for example the 4th Company of the 40th Regiment lost twenty-five men to a single round shot.[20]

Common Shell: This was a hollow cast-iron sphere, of the same diameter as round shot for any given gun, which was filled with gunpowder and fitted with a fuse. This, a wooden plug containing a train of gunpowder, was ignited by the flash of the hot gases from the main charge as the gun was fired, and the length of burning time of the fuse could be varied to some extent in the hope that the charge would explode near the target, flinging fragments of shell casing into the enemy.

Canister or Case Shot: A number of lead balls were packed into a cylindrical tin container which, when fired, split open allowing the balls to spread out, in effect turning the cannon into a giant shotgun. Because the balls spread out quite widely over a comparatively short distance canister had a maximum effective range of about three hundred yards, but it was generally used over much shorter ranges, often when the artillery position was being directly threatened by an enemy force, particularly cavalry. There are recorded instances of artillery in this situation loading with two rounds of canister, or one round shot and one canister, to ward off an attack.

Shrapnel Shell: This type of ammunition was used only by British artillery during the Peninsular campaign and at Waterloo. It had been invented by General Henry Shrapnel in 1785, and consisted of a hollow cast-iron sphere similar to that of the common shell, but containing a number of lead balls, a bursting charge of gunpowder, and a fuse. This shell was intended to burst in the air and release the lead balls, which, following the trajectory of the shell, would fall on the enemy. With a particular target in mind it was of course essential that the burning-time of the fuse was set absolutely accurately, a difficult task, particularly in battlefield conditions, but there is some evidence that it was found quite effective in its use against the French forces.

Ammunition for the 6 pdr gun: The top illustration shows (left to right); i) a canvas cartridge contained a standard charge of $1\frac{1}{2}$ lbs of gunpowder, ii) a round shot, and iii) a round of canister shot. At bottom left is a round of common shell, cut in half to show its fuse and its bursting charge of coarse gunpowder. At bottom right is a similarly sectioned round of Shrapnel shell.

This ammunition is all in the Museum of Artillery in the Rotunda, Woolwich.

A note on *Grape Shot*: this is often referred to both by contemporary and later writers as having been used by land service artillery during the Peninsula and at Waterloo. Grape takes its name from the fact that it was made up of usually nine large iron balls grouped or 'bunched' about a heavy iron spike projecting from a wooden disc, the balls generally fastened by a canvas bag bound with wire. On firing, grape operated like very heavy canister.

Despite the references mentioned, however, there is no official record of the issue of grape shot to British land service artillery during the Napoleonic wars, indeed the only mention in contemporary documents is of its undesirability due to the rapid wear it would cause to the bores of brass guns. Grape, therefore, was purely a naval round, since it would do little harm to the iron ordnance of that service. The likely explanation for the misuse of

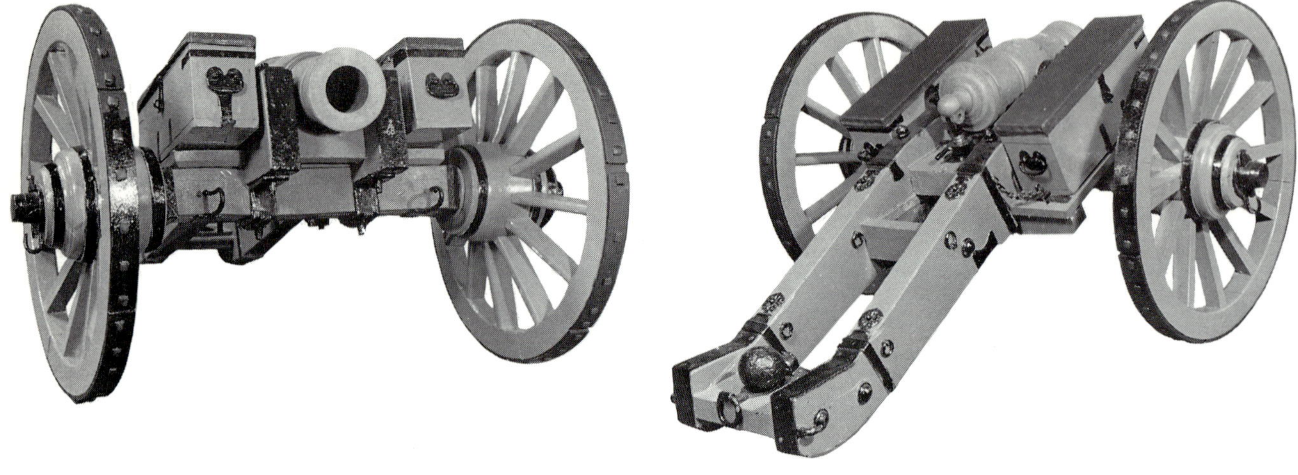

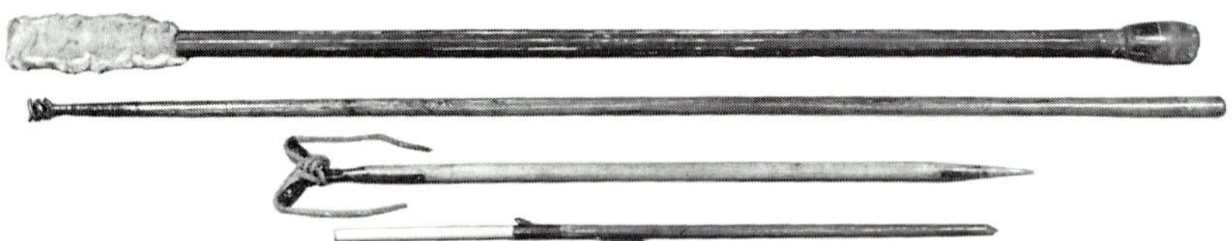

A standard $5\frac{1}{2}$ inch light howitzer of the Napoleonic wars.
The barrel, which weighs four hundredweights and which is just over two feet in length, was cast by P. Verbruggen at Woolwich in 1782. The carriage is an exact copy of an original. The illustration on the right shows the double-bracket trail common to all British artillery until the introduction of the Congreve carriage for light guns.

BOTTOM: Loading and firing implements. (Top to bottom): i) a sponge-staff and rammer, ii) a worm for clearing the bore of obstructions, iii) a linstock fitted with a length of match cord, and, iv) a portfire in its wooden holder.

These pieces are all in the Museum of Artillery in the Rotunda, Woolwich.

the term is that there were two types of canister shot issued; light and heavy. Both rounds weighed approximately the same (for a 6 pdr gun about 8 lb) but the balls within the 'heavy' canister were roughly twice the size of those within the 'light' and were correspondingly fewer in number. It is possible that heavy canister was referred to as 'grape' by contemporary gunners purely as a convenience to differentiate it from light canister shot.

Having outlined the ammunition available to field guns it is important to mention the other vital part of field artillery of our period; the howitzer. In contrast to the gun which had a relatively long barrel (usually between fourteen and twenty-four times the diameter of its bore) for greatest muzzle velocity and flattest trajectory, the howitzer had a barrel of only four to six times its bore diameter. Unlike the gun it was designed to fire its projectiles in a curved trajectory in order that it could, for instance, fire over the heads of advancing friendly troops to aid their attack.[21] Round shot or canister were largely ineffective when fired in this way, thus the howitzer almost invariably fired an explosive round, either common or shrapnel shell.

Unlike the gun the howitzer was described by its bore diameter rather than by the weight of its projectile. The howitzers in British field service had bores of $4\frac{1}{2}$ and $5\frac{1}{2}$ inches and were generally mounted on double-bracket carriages. During the Napoleonic wars British field batteries were usually composed of five 6 or 9 pdr guns and one howitzer.

Despite the state of relative sophistication which smooth-bore artillery had reached by the early nineteenth century, the firing procedure of a muzzle-loading piece had to be followed absolutely as laid down in the drill manual if a serious accident to a member of the detachment was to be avoided. The danger lay in the possible premature ignition of the main charge, and the following sequence was designed to minimise risk as far as possible:

The minimum number in a detachment to safely handle a gun was five; an NCO, who usually stood behind the trail of the carriage and who aimed the piece and directed operations, the 'ventsman' on the right side of the breech and the 'firer' on the left, and the 'spongeman' and 'loader' on each side of the muzzle.

The first action after the gun had been fired was for the spongeman to dip the sponge on the end of his combined sponge-staff and rammer into a bucket of water and thoroughly swab out the bore, to extinguish any glowing fragments of the previous charge and to cleanse the bore of powder fouling. The loader then placed the new charge, a fabric bag or 'cartridge' containing a measured load of gunpowder, followed by the chosen projectile, in the muzzle of the piece. The spongeman then reversed the staff to present its wooden head to the muzzle, but before the charge could be safely rammed home the ventsman had to cover the vent or touch-hole of the gun with a leather thumb-stall. This action (known as 'serving the vent') prevented a rush of air through the vent, which might fan any glowing fragments of charge not extinguished by the sponge, thereby igniting the charge as it was being rammed, with obvious dire consequences for the unfortunate spongeman. With the charge safely rammed home the ventsman would thrust a pointed rod or 'pricker' down the vent to pierce the fabric cartridge to aid ignition, and a primer, in the form of a quill tube filled with fine gunpowder, was placed in the vent. The gun was fired by a device called a 'portfire'; a paper tube about three-quarters of an inch in diameter and eighteen inches long, filled with a composition which burned at a rate of about an inch a minute, and for safety mounted in a wooden handle. When action was imminent the firer lit the portfire from a piece of burning match-cord held in a 'linstock', a staff about four feet long which was placed in the ground at the gun position and which was a source of fire throughout the length of an engagement. Having lit the portfire from the linstock and fired the gun the burning end of the portfire was removed by the use of a portfire cutter, a simple guillotine device usually permanently attached to the trail of the carriage.

Rates of fire: it is very difficult to gather an accurate impression of rates of artillery fire from actions of the Peninsula campaign and at Waterloo. It was possible for a well-drilled detachment, in ideal circumstances, to achieve a rate of fire of up to eight rounds per minute, but in battle there were many factors which could drastically reduce this remarkable number: Simply to safeguard the men a slower rate of fire was insisted upon in order that the gun should not overheat and that the loading and firing sequence should be properly followed; the gun position itself might not be ideal and re-laying the gun after each firing might take longer than in practice; there might well be losses within the detachment itself; but probably a very great delaying factor would be the simple fact that often the gun crews would be unable to see their target due to the enormous quantity of dense white smoke, generated not only by their own guns but by every other firearm on the battlefield.

Tactics: there is really too little space within this chapter to deal properly with this topic;[22] however, it is true to say that, wherever possible, British field gun batteries were placed on the flanks of the troops they were supporting, in order that they could fire at as acute an angle as possible along the enemy lines. This technique, called 'enfilade' fire, used the gun's flat trajectory to greatest effect, round shot often causing the great number of casualties to which we have already alluded.

A last point to be mentioned regarding the armament of the British field artillery during the period under discussion is really a rather minor one; the use of explosive rockets.

A large military rocket had been devised in 1805 by Colonel Sir William Congreve (son of the inventor of the block-trail gun carriage). This device had a head some two feet long armed with either a round shot or shell and attached to a stick whose length would vary between eight and ten feet, the length of stick controlling the trajectory of the rocket once launched.

The Congreve rocket was first tried in anger at Copenhagen in 1807 and was quite successful, but three years later, at Santarem in the Peninsula, the erratic behaviour of the rockets, which would sometimes turn back and land uncomfortably near those who had launched them, apparently displeased Lord Wellington, who said he would prefer to use 9 pdr guns.

Little more is heard of rockets until 1813, by which time Rocket Troops had been formed within the Royal Horse Artillery, when the rockets of the 2nd Troop were used to good effect upon the massed French formations at the battle of Leipzig. In the following year rockets were tried again at Toulouse and on the Adour, when a small detachment beat off at close range an attack by some French cavalry, more apparently by frightening the horses, which had a healthy dislike for rocket fire, than by actual damage.

Probably the best known instance of the use of rockets during our period, however, is during the Waterloo campaign, when on 17th June 1815, at Genappe, Captain Whinyate's Troop, RHA, engaged at short range a battery of French horse artillery. The action began well enough, with the first rocket scoring a direct hit and driving the French detachments from their guns, but this success was marred by subsequent rockets returning with the unpredictable 'boomerang' effect which was such as unfortunate characteristic of Congreve's design.

Congreve rockets curving through the air at Waterloo. Wellington was scornful of this weapon and it was little used in the battle.

OVERLEAF: Wellington's funeral procession passing Apsley House. The grandiose catafalque, specially constructed for the occasion with metal from the Duke's captured guns, may still be inspected at Stratfield Saye.

At Waterloo itself some fifty-eight rockets are recorded as having been fired, apparently with some effect, though the standing crops tended to muffle their impact. In all it cannot be said that rocketry played a significant role at any time during the Napoleonic wars.[23]

PLACE
3
BROM

The Authors

CORRELLI BARNETT is keeper of the Archives at Churchill College, Cambridge, and has written numerous interpretive – and sometimes controversial – military histories. These include *The Desert Generals* (1960), *The Swordbearers* (1963), and *Bonaparte* (1978). He was part-author of the television series *The Great War* and author of *The Lost Peace* and *The Commanders* series.

MICHAEL GLOVER saw action in the Second World War and subsequently served with the British Council until 1970. He is noted for his scholarly studies of Wellington and the Peninsular War, including *Wellington's Peninsular Victories* (1963), *Wellington as Military Commander* (1968) and *The Peninsular War* (1974).

PADDY GRIFFITH is a senior lecturer in War Studies at the Royal Military Academy, Sandhurst. His books include *Forward Into Battle* (1981) and (with Elmar Dinter) *Not Over by Christmas* (1983). He has also written extensively on war gaming.

DAVID HOWARTH started his career with the BBC, then served in the RNVR during the Second World War, when he was decorated twice by the Norwegian government. Since then he has been a prolific author in many fields; as novelist, biographer, children's author and writer on the 'secret war' 1939–45. Among his best known works of military history are *Trafalgar – The Nelson Touch* (1969), *1066: Year of the Conquest* (1977) and – on Waterloo – *A Near Run Thing* (1968).

JOHN KEEGAN is a senior lecturer in War Studies at the Royal Military Academy, Sandhurst. His numerous books on military subjects include *Waffen SS, the Asphalt Soldiers* (1970), *World Armies* (1979) and *Six Armies in Normandy* (1982), although he is probably best known for *The Face of Battle* (1976). He has recently been part-author of the television series *Soldiers*.

GRAEME RIMER has since 1975 been a member of staff in the Department of Firearms in the Armouries, HM Tower of London. He has written extensively on firearms subjects and is Editor of the *Journal* of the Society of Arms and Armour.

JOHN TERRAINE was a BBC producer until 1963, since when he has written more than a dozen works of military history, including *Douglas Haig, the Educated Soldier* (1963), *The Western Front* (1964) and *The Smoke and the Fire* (1980). He was chief script writer for *The Great War* and *The Mighty Continent* television series, among others.

Appendix – Wellington's Campaigns

Approximate statistics for some of Wellington's major military transactions. (Note that in many cases these are no more than guesswork.) 1) A blank entry implies that *combat* casualties were negligible, not that there were no overall casualties. (Eg. Massena suffered 25,000 in Portugal, 1810–11, but very few in combat.) 2) losses include all casualties, deaths and prisoners taken. 3) KGL = King's German Legion.

Event	Date	Enemy Commander	Enemy Numbers	Enemy Losses
Seringapatam campaign (Wellington was subordinate to Harris)	1799	Tipoo Sahib	50,000(?)	10,000(?)
Battle of Assaye	1803	Scindia/Berar	60,000(+)	3,000(?)
Battle of Argaum	1803	Scindia/Berar	40,000(?)	10,000(?)
Battle of Köge	1807	Castenskjold	14,000	2,000(?)
Battle of Vimeiro	1808	Junot	13,000	2,000
Battle of Oporto	1809	Soult	11,000	1,000(?)
Battle of Talavera	1809	Jourdan/Victor	46,000	7,300
Non-battle of Almaraz	1809	Soult/Ney	45,000	—
Battle of Busaco	1810	Massena	66,000	4,500
Non-battle of Santarem/Sobral	1810	Massena	50,000	—
Battle of Fuentes de Oñoro	1811	Massena	48,000	2,200
Non-battle of the Caia	1811	Soult/Marmont	60,000	—
Non-battle of Fuenteguinaldo/El Bodon	1811	Marmont	60,000	200
1st Non-battle of San Christoval	1812	Marmont	40–50,000	100(?)
Battle of Salamanca	1812	Marmont	50,000	14,000(?)
Advance to Burgos	1812	Clausel	25,000(?)	—
Retreat from Burgos	1812	Clausel/Souham	53,000	—
2nd Non-battle of San Christoval	1812	Soult	80,000	—
Battle of Vitoria	1813	Joseph/Jourdan	66,000	8,000
Battles of Pyrenees	1813	Soult	53,000	13,500
Battle of Nive/Nivelle (4 months' action)	1813	Soult	86,000	15,000(+)
Battle of Orthez	1814	Soult	40,000	4,500
Battle of Toulouse	1814	Soult	42,000	4,000
Battle of Quatre Bras	1815	Ney	23,000(?)	4,400
Battle of Waterloo	1815	Ney/Napoleon	72,000	37,000(?)

Wellington's force Numbers	British/KGL present	British/KGL as per cent of allies	British/KGL as per cent of enemy	Total losses to Wellington's force	Allied losses as percentage of allied total
57,000	7,000	13%	14%	1,500(?)	2.6%
12,000(?)	5,000(−)	43%	8%	1,800(?)	15.0%
18,000	5,000(−)	28%	12%	400(?)	2.2%
5,000	5,000	100%	35%	300(?)	6.0%
17,000	17,000	100%	140%	750	4.4%
initially 600	600	100%	6%	150	25.0%
55,000	21,000	38%	45%	5,400	9.8%
30,000(?)	18,000	60%	41%	—	—
51,000	31,000	60%	46%	1,200	2.3%
61,000	40,000	62%	80%	—	—
38,000	27,000	77%	53%	1,600	4.2%
44,000	30,000(?)	68%	50%	—	—
46,000	32,000(?)	71%	53%	200	—
48,000	28,000	59%	62%	100	—
49,000	30,000	59%	60%	5,200	10.6%
30,000(?)	14,000(?)	47%	56%	—	—
34,000	14,000(?)	41%	25%	—	—
70,000	33,000(?)	48%	41%	—	—
79,000	37,000	46%	55%	5,200	6.5%
40,000	23,000(?)	58%	44%	7,100	17.7%
89,000	40,000(?)	44%	45%	11,000(+)	12.3%
44,000	30,000(?)	68%	75%	2,200	5.0%
46,000	25,000(?)	56%	60%	5,400	11.7%
30,000(?)	8,000(?)	27%	35%	4,500	9.8%
68,000 + 80,000 Prussians	30,000	45% (20%) Prussians	43%	15,000(?) +7,000 Prussians	22.0% (14.2%) Prussians

Notes

The following abbreviations are used for works most frequently cited in the footnotes throughout the book:

Napier: Napier, W. F. P., *History of the War in the Peninsula* (6 vols., Boone, London 1862)

Oman: Oman, C., *History of the Peninsular War* (7 vols, Oxford U.P., 1902–30)

SD: *Supplementary Despatches and Memoranda of the Duke of Wellington* ed. Second Duke of Wellington (14 vols, 1858–72)

Selections: *Selections from the Dispatches and General Orders of Field Marshal the Duke of Wellington* ed. J. Gurwood (Murray, London 1841)

Ward: Ward, S. G. P., *Wellington* (Batsford, London 1963)

WD: *The Despatches of the Field Marshal the Duke of Wellington* ed. J. Gurwood (12 vols. 1834–39)

Wellington-Commander

1. The second half of the twentieth century has seen no apparent slackening in the output of Wellington studies. Most useful among recent works are S. G. P. Ward's magnificent pair of books – *Wellington* (*op cit*) and *Wellington's Headquarters* (Oxford U. P., 1957); Michael Glover's perceptive *Wellington as Military Commander* (Batsford, London 1968); and his *Wellington's Pensinsular Victories* (Batsford 1963), *Wellington's Army in the Peninsula* (David & Charles, Newton Abbot 1977), &c. From the American weapons expert Jac Weller we have a trilogy of successively more mature narratives – *Wellington in the Peninsula* (N. Vane, London 1962), *Wellington at Waterloo* (Longman, London 1967) and *Wellington in India* (Longman, London 1972). Godfrey Davies' *Wellington and his Army* (Blackwell, Oxford 1954) contains some controversial essays on the Duke's character, while Antony Brett-James' *Wellington at War* (Macmillan, London 1961) is an excellent modern selection from his correspondence. Not centrally concerned with Wellington, but indispensable for Waterloo are H. T. Siborne's *Waterloo Letters* (Cassel, London 1891 and re-issued 1983).

2. Gleig, G. R., *The Subaltern* (Blackwoods, Edinburgh 1872) p. 67.

3. Cited in Oman vol 7 p. 251.

4. Selections p. 905.

5. Wellington was baptised Arthur Wesley but from 1798 followed his elder brother in spelling his name 'Wellesley'. In 1805 he was created a supplementary Knight of the Bath, while in 1809, after Talavera, he became Baron Douro of Wellesley and Viscount Wellington of Talavera. The taking of Ciudad Rodrigo in 1812 was rewarded by an earldom; the battle of Salamanca by a marquessate, and it was ironically after the retreat from Burgos that he joined the Order of the Garter. Vitoria saw him promoted Field Marshal and after Napoleon's first abdication in 1814 he finally became a Duke. For simplicity, however, I have stuck to 'Wellington' throughout, although in India he will be referred to as Arthur Wellesley.

6. Selections p. 481. We should never underestimate the extent to which nineteenth-century military institutions, no less than professional, governmental or trade union institutions, were still in their 'mythic' or 'personal' stage of development. They had not yet achieved the 'banality' and massively regimented character which has marked them in more recent times. Much postwar military sociology has examined the latter phase of this transition, but little attention has been paid to the former. Compare the trade union experience as in eg. Mouriaux, R., *Les Syndicats dans la Société Française* (Sciences Politiques press, Paris 1983) pp. 13, 224 &c.

7. From Croker papers, 14th June 1808, cited in Oman's *Wellington's Army* (Arnold, London 1912) p. 79. This passage has often been wrongly used as a reference for Wellington's minor tactics, when in fact it refers to his grand tactics.

8. Cited in Brett-James, *op cit* p. 159, *n*. Compare another of Wellington's comments – 'The battle of Talavera was certainly the hardest fought of modern days . . .' (*Ibid* p. 179).

9. Selections p. 297 shows Wellington, on 6th October 1809, talking of an evacuation 'whenever' rather than 'if ever' it should be necessary.

10. Selections p. 477.

11. *Ibid* p. 542.

12. *Ibid* p. 593.

13. *Ibid* p. 609.

14. Tomkinson, W., *Diary of a Cavalry Officer* ed. J. Tomkinson (London 1894) p. 188, records that Wellington was exceptionally nervous that morning. I am especially grateful to Michael Glover for drawing my attention to this and many other points of detail on the Peninsular War.

15. Selections p. 651.

16. *Ibid* p. 723.

17. Ward p. 99.
18. Napoleon at Waterloo fits even better into the *War and Peace* stereotype of generalship than Wellington. Note also that the 'tide of history' at Waterloo had already been vividly described by Stendhal in the 1830's, in *La Chartreuse de Parme.*

Wellington as an Attacking General – the Peninsular War

1. WD vol 4 p. 430. Wellington to Castlereagh, 17th June 1809.
2. WD vol 4 p. 412. Wellington to Villiers, 11th June 1809.
3. *Memoirs and Literary Remains of Lt. Gen. Sir H. E. Bunbury* (privately printed 1868) p. 295.
4. SD vol 8 p. 147. Melville to Wellington, 28th July 1813.
5. Stanhope MS., quoted in Fortuescue's *History of the British Army* vol 7 p. 547.
6. *Ibid* vol 8 p. 462.
7. WD vol 11 p. 40. Wellington to Bentinck, 25th August 1813.
8. *Private Journal of Judge Advocate Larpent* ed. G. Larpent (3rd edition, London 1854) p. 168: Undated letter of (?) 2nd July 1813.
9. *Conversations of the Duke of Wellington with G. W. Chad* ed. seventh Duke (London), 1956) p. 2.
10. WD vol 4 p. 303. Wellington to Beresford, 6th May 1809.
11. SD vol 6 p. 582. Wellington to Torrens, 29th August 1810.
12. SD vol 7 p. 494. Wellington to Torrens, 6th December 1812.
13. *Report on the Manuscripts of Earl Bathurst*, Historical Manuscripts Commission, 1923. Wellington to Bathurst, 30th October 1814.
14. *The Croker Papers* ed. L. W. Jennings (3 vols, London 1884) vol 2 p. 123.
15. SD vol 6 p. 582. Wellington to Torrens, 29th August 1810.
16. Quoted in Fortescue, vol 7 p. 419. Torrens to Wellington, 11th September 1810.
17. *Vie Militaire du Général Foy* ed. Girod de l'Ain (Paris, 1900) p. 178.
18. WD vol 10 p. 372. Wellington to Bathurst, 11th May 1813.
19. WE vol 10 p. 613. Wellington to Bathurst, 8th August 1813.

Wellington as a Coalition General

1. Dwight D. Eisenhower, *Crusade in Europe* (Heinemann 1948) p. 175.
2. Ward p. 46.
3. Philip Mason, *A Matter of Honour* (Cape, London 1974) p. 155 – in a section entitled 'Wellesley Bahadur'.
4. Richard Aldington, *Wellington* (Heinemann 1946) p. 80.
5. *Ibid* p. 81.
6. Ward p. 63.
7. Napier vol 5 p. 346.
8. Oman vol 1 pp. 101–2.
9. Napier vol 2 p. 150.
10. Philip Guedalla, *The Duke* (Hodder & Stoughton, London 1946) p. 184.
11. Oman, vol 2 p. 514. Wellesley to Castlereagh, 25th August 1809, *n.*
12. Napier vol 2 p. 154.
13. Aldington, *op cit*, p. 141.
14. Oman, vol 2 p. 310 *n.*
15. Cotton, Sgt. Maj. E., *A Voice from Waterloo* (Briard, Brussels 1862) p. 259.

Playing Into His Hands – Bonaparte"s Mistakes

1. I refer throughout *not* to the so-called and self-appointed 'Emperor Napoleon', but to 'Bonaparte'. This was Wellington's own way, and I am happy to follow it.

For further details of the career of Bonaparte, the reader is referred to my book of that name (George Allen & Unwin, London 1978).

The best purely military analysis of the Waterloo campaign is: Lieut-Colonel Charles C. Chesney R E *Waterloo Lectures: A Study of the Campaign of 1815* (London 1868).

The Myth of the Thin Red Line

1. William Howard Russell, *Russell's Despatches from the Crimea* ed. N. Bentley (Panther edn., 1970) p. 122. For Russell's career, see Knightley, P., *The First Casualty: the war correspondent as hero, propagandist and myth maker from the Crimea to Vietnam* (London 1975).
2. Creasy, E. S., *Fifteen Decisive Battles of the World* ed. A. Butler (Everyman edn., London 1963) pp. 383–4 and 386.
3. The classic case was perhaps that of the 42nd and 44th regiments at Quatre Bras, but there were other instances at Sabugal and El Bodon in 1811. See Oman, *Wellington's Army* (*op. cit.*) p. 99.
4. Bas, F. de, *et al.*, *La Campagne de 1815 aux Pays-Bas* (3 vols., Brussels 1909) Vol. 2 p. 135 and Vol. 3 p. 339, for a discussion of Bijlandt's role in halting d'Erlon's early attacks. In Vol. 2 pp. 271–9 the importance of Dettmer's intervention against the Imperial Guard at the end of the day is stressed. De Bas is a magnificent source for many aspects of the battle, but in these two cases his account runs directly counter to the British view of the matter.
5. Selections p. 288.
6. Hibbert, C., ed., *A Soldier of the Seventy-First* (Cooper, London 1975) p. 60. I am especially grateful to Ned Zuparko for drawing my attention to this passage, and to those cited in footnotes 8 and 11. See his *Charges, Firefights and Morale* in *Empires, Eagles and Lions* magazines Nos. 70–71, March & April 1983. This journal is an indispensable aid to any studies in Napoleonic tactical history; available from R A F M, 19 Concession St., Cambridge, Ontario, Canada N1R 2G6.
7. Siborne's *Waterloo Letters* (*op. cit.*) p. 340.
8. Hennell, G., *A Gentleman Volunteer* ed. M. Glover (Heinemann, London 1979) p. 31.
9. *Ibid*, p. 136.
10. While it is true that the 93rd wasted their first volley, it is also true that the range of their rifle-muskets in 1854 was very greatly superior to that of Wellington's firelocks in 1815. A different tactical philosophy was arguably justifiable with the new long-range weapons.
11. Wheeler, W., *The Letters of Private Wheeler* ed. B. H. Liddell Hart (London 1951) p. 86.
12. Aitchison, J., *An Ensign in the Peninsular War* ed. W.F.K. Thompson (Joseph, London 1981) p. 58.

13. The best succinct analysis of Wellington's tribulations in this period is in Ward. For Wellington's 'spirit of the bayonet' in India read Weller's *Wellington in India* (op. cit.).

14. See my own *Forward Into Battle* (Bird, Chichester 1981) for a discussion of this point.

15. Curling, H., ed., *Recollections of Rifleman Harris* (Davies, London 1929) p. 24.

16. One possible motive for riflemen picking off enemy officers was explained to Capt. Landmann, RE, at Vimeiro by a German sharpshooter of the 60th. This man explained why he did not wish to shoot a French skirmisher who was seen at 60–80 yards' range: " 'Silence!", he said, "Ton't tisturp me; I want de officer." "Why?", asked Landmann. "Pecause ter pe more plunder." ' (Landmann, *Recollections of my Military Life*, Hurst & Blackett, London 1854, Vol. 2, p. 221).

On the other hand there seems to have been a distinct tendency on the part of French officers to place themselves at the points of maximum danger, and to stand firm when their men fled. This must naturally have led to disproportionate casualties. See Oman, C., *Column and Line in the Peninsula* in *Studies in the Napoleonic Wars* (London 1929) p. 107, where he favours this view rather than the 'rifle' interpretation.

For battlefield duelling, see Oman's *History of the Peninsular War* Vol. 6 p. 295, for Captain Waldron at Castalla.

17. Everard, H., *History of Thomas Farrington's Regiment, 1694–1891* (Worcester 1891) p. 278.

The Weapons of Wellington's Army

1. John Keegan, *The Face of Battle*, London, 1976.

2. For a fuller description of these muskets see H. L. Blackmore; 'British Military Firearms', London, 1961, pp. 96 & 105.

3. See W.J. Carman: *Infantry Clothing Regulations, 1802*, Journal of the Society of Army Historical Research, (JSAHR), Vol. XIX (1940). I am grateful to Mr Michael Baldwin formerly of the National Army Museum, London, for drawing my attention to this article.

4. Colonel G. Hanger, *Colonel George Hanger to all Sportsmen*, London, 1814, p. 205.

5. Hans Busk, *The Rifle and How to Use It*, 6th edition, London 1860, p. 17.

6. Major-General B. P. Hughes, C.B., C.B.E.; *Firepower, Weapons effectiveness on the battlefield, 1630–1850*, London 1974.

7. Ezekiel Baker, *Remarks on Rifle Guns*, London 1835, pp. 90–94.

8. In 1792 it was ordered that sergeants of infantry should be issued with spontoons, as a weapon and as a badge of rank, and these were certainly carried throughout the Napoleonic Wars. Sergeants' fusils were also issued, however, and we cannot be sure what proportion of sergeants carried which arm. The Spontoon was not officially laid aside until 1830.

9. See Brian Robson; *Swords of the British Army. The Regulation Patterns 1788–1914*, London 1975, pp. 108–14.

10. For a biography of Le Marchant see R. H. Thoumine, *Scientific Soldier, A Life of General Le Marchant, 1766–1812*, London 1968.

11. Ibid., p. 17.

12. Robson, op. cit., pp. 14–22.

13. Ibid., p. 26.

14. Lt. Col. William Tomkinson; *The Diary of a Cavalry Officer in the Peninsular and Waterloo Campaigns 1809–1815*, London 1895, p. 114.

15. i) For the use of the lance by the French cavalry at Waterloo see Keegan, op. cit., pp. 146, 150, 151, & 202–3.

ii) For an engagement between the 14th Light Dragoons and a company of Polish lancers in 1811 see Colonel H. B. Hamilton, *Historical Record of the 14th (King's) Hussars*, London 1901, pp. 90–1.

16. I am grateful to Mr De Witt Bailey for this information.

17. For more detailed information see Keegan, op. cit., pp. 147–60.

18. This incident is mentioned by Keegan, op. cit., p. 155.

19. William Müller for example (see Hughes, op. cit., p. 29).

20. See Keegan, op. cit., p. 161.

21. i) For a diagram of the designed trajectory of shrapnel shells see Hughes, op. cit., p. 34.

ii) Shrapnel shell was used to support infantry at Waterloo, for example, Keegan, op. cit., p. 162.

22 Again, see Hughes, op. cit. for a larger scale study.

23 i) For notes on Rocket Troops in British service see Major G. Tylden, *The Use of War Rockets in the British Army in the Nineteenth Century*, JSAHR, Vol. 26, (1948) pp. 168–170.

ii) For the history and development of Congreve's military rockets and of the establishment of a Rocket Troop in 1814 see Colonel William Congreve; *The Details of the Rocket System*, London 1814.

Bibliography

A short selection of further reading for the subjects covered in this book:—

Aldington, R., *Wellington* (London, 1946)

Baker, E., *Remarks on Rifle Guns* (11th edn., London, 1835)

Barnett, C., *Bonaparte* (London, 1978)

Beatson, F. C., *Wellington: The Bidassoa and Nivelle* (London, 1931)

Beatson, F. C., *With Wellington in the Pyrenees* (London, n.d. - 1914?)

Blackmore, *British Military Firearms, 1650–1850* (London, 1961)

Brett-James, A., *Wellington at War, 1794–1815* (London, 1961)

Busk, H., *The Rifle and How to Use It* (6th edn., London 1860)

Carman, W. J., *Infantry Clothing Regulations, 1802* in *Journal of the Society of Army Historical Research*, Vol XIX (1940)

Chalfont, Lord, *Waterloo: Battle of Three Armies* (London, 1979)

Chesney, C. Lt. Col., *Waterloo Lectures: A study of the Campaign of 1815* (London, 1868)

Congreve, W., *The Details of the Rocket System* (London, 1814)

Davies, G., *Wellington and his Army* (Oxford, 1954)

Fortescue, J. W., *History of the British Army* (13 vols, London, 1899–1930)

Glover, M., *The Peninsular War* (Newton Abbot, 1974)

Glover, M., *Wellington's Army in the Peninsula* (Newton Abbot, 1977)

Glover, M., *Wellington as Military Commander* (London, 1968)

Glover, M., *Wellington's Peninsular Victories* (London, 1963)

Glover, R., *Peninsular Preparation, the Reform of the British Army, 1795–1809* (Cambridge, 1963)

Griffith, P.G., *Forward Into Battle* (Chichester, 1981)

Gurwood, J., ed., *The Dispatches of the Field Marshal the Duke of Wellington* (12 vols., London, 1834–9)

Gurwood, J., ed. *Selections from the Dispatches and General Orders of Field Marshal the Duke of Wellington* (London, 1841)

Guedalla, P., *The Duke* (new edn., London, 1946)

Hanger, G., *Col. George Hanger to All Sportsmen and Particularly to Farmers and Gamekeepers* (London, 1814)

Horward, D. D., *The Battle of Bussaco* (Tallhassee, 1965)

Howarth, D., *A Near Run Thing* (London, 1968)

Hughes, B. P., *British Smoothbore Artillery* (London, 1969)

Hughes, B. P. *Open fire – Artillery Tactics from Marlborough to Wellington* (Chichester, 1983)

Jennings, L. W., ed., *The Croker Papers* (3 vols, London, 1884)

Keegan, J., *The Face of Battle* (London, 1976)

Larpent, G., ed. *Private Journal of Judge Advocate Larpent* (3rd edn., London, 1854)

Longford, E., *Wellington: Pillar of State* (London, 1972)

Longford, E., *Wellington, the Years of the Sword* (London, 1969)

Maxwell, H., *The Life of Wellington* (2 vols., London, 1900)

Napier, W. F. P., *History of the War in the Peninsula* (6 vols., new edn., London, 1862)

Naylor, J., *Waterloo* (London, 1960)

Oman, C., *History of the Peninsular War* (7 vols., Oxford, 1902–30)

Oman, C., *Studies in the Napoleonic Wars* (London, 1929)

Oman, C., *Wellington's Army* (London, 1912)

Robson, B., *Swords of the British Army. The Regulation Patterns 1788–1914* (London, 1975)

Rogers, H. C. B., *Weapons of the British Soldier* (London, 1960)

Rogers, H. C. B., *Wellington's Army* (London, 1979)

Siborne, H. T., *Waterloo Letters* (London, 1891 reissued 1983)

Stanhope, P. H., *Notes on Conversations with the Duke of Wellington* (new edn., Oxford, 1938)

Terraine, J., *Right Good Captains* in *British Army Review*, no. 67, April, 1981, p. 16.

Thoumine, R.H., *Scientific Soldier, A Life of General Le Marchant, 1766–1812* (London, 1968)

Tomkinson, W., *The Diary of a Cavalry Officer in the Peninsular and Waterloo Campaigns 1809–1815* (London, 1895)

Tulard, J., *Napoléon, ou le Mythe du Sauveur* (Paris, 1977)

Ward, S. G. P., *Wellington* (London, 1963)

Ward, S. G. P., *Wellington's Headquarters* (Oxford, 1957)

Weller, J., *Wellington in India* (London, 1972)

Weller, J., *Wellington in the Peninsula* (London, 1962)

Weller, J., *Wellington at Waterloo* (London, 1967)

Wellesley, M., *The Man Wellington Through the Eyes of Those Who Knew Him* (London, 1937)

Second Duke of Wellington, ed., *Supplementary Despatches and Memoranda of the Duke of Wellington* (14 vols., London, 1858–72)

7th Duke of Wellington, ed., *Conversations of the Duke of Wellington with G. W. Chad* (Cambridge, 1956)

7th Duke of Wellington, ed., *Wellington and his Friends* (London, 1965)

Illustration Acknowledgements

Despite diligent enquiries it has not been possible to trace the owners of some of the illustrations in this book. Our apologies are due to those copyright holders who can substantiate their claims. In application the Publishers they will receive usual fee for reproduction.

The following abbreviations are used for the major sources of illustration: National Army Museum (*NAM*); National Portrait Gallery (*NPG*); Victoria and Albert Museum (*V & A*).

reverse of frontispiece The Wellington Shield, designed by Thomas Stothard RA and made by Benjamin Smith. *V & A*

frontispiece Portrait of Wellington by Goya. *NPG*

page 6–7 Apsley House in early Victorian Times. *V & A*

8–9 The Waterloo banquet at Apsley House. *V & A*

12 Formal portrait of Wellington by J. Hoppner. *By permission of the Duke of Wellington, Stratfield Saye: photograph Courtauld Institute of Art*

15 Wellington as Lieutenant Colonel of the 33rd Foot, by J. Hoppner. *By permission of the Duke of Wellington, Stratfield Saye: photograph Courtauld Institute of Art*

16 (*facing*) The Waterloo Gallery by Joseph Nash at Apsley House. *V & A*

17 (*facing*) Wellington encouraging a square at Waterloo, by R. A. Hillingford. *By courtesy of Christie's London and the Bridgeman Art Library*

18 General Sir George Murray, by John Prescott Knight RA. *V & A*

19 (*above*) Sir David Baird. Engraving by Burnet after Wilkie. *NPG*
(*below*) Captain Ramsey RHA saving the guns of Bull's Troop at Fuentes de Onoro. *Parker Gallery*

22 Cavalry charge at Assaye, by Abraham Cooper RA. *Parker Gallery*

23 Crossing the Bidassoa by W. Heath. *V & A*

24 Landing troops from ship. Aquatint by M. Duborg after J. A. Atkinson. *NAM*

25 General Lord Hill, by C. Smith. *NPG*

27 The storming of Gawilghur by J. Duplesis Bertaux. *V & A*

30 (*left*) General Junot, by Raverat. *Bulloz, photo copyright; Musée de l'Armée, Paris*
(*right*) Sir John Moore, by T. Lawrence. *NPG*

33 The ridge at Busaco. *Paddy Griffith*

34 The brook at Fuentes de Onoro. *Paddy Griffith*

35 Marshal Marmont, by Guerin. *Bulloz, photo copyright*; Versailles

36 The Siege of Badajoz, by H. Leveque. *NAM*

37 (*above*) Badajoz today. *Paddy Griffith*
(*below*) Badajoz: the St Christobal outworks. *Paddy Griffith*

38 The storming of Badajoz, by J. Duplessis Bertaux. *V & A*

39 Surrender of the keys of Madrid. *V & A*

40 (*above*) Marching French prisoners into Salamanca. Aquatint by Clark and Duborg after Capt. Wilmot RHA. *NAM*
(*below*) Salamanca, by R. Simkin. *NAM*

41 The French 'Arapiles' at Salamaca. *Paddy Griffith*

42–43 Wellington, by Goya. *V & A*

44 Incident in the battle of vitoria, by J. Atkinson. *By permission of the Duke of Wellington, Stratfield Saye: photograph Courtauld Institute of Art*

45 (*above*) Pamplona. *Paddy Griffith*
(*below left*) The battlefield of Sorauren. *Paddy Griffith*
(*below right*) The hill stormed by Wellington at Sorauren. *Paddy Griffith*

47 Wellington crossing the Pyrenees. Oil by T. J. Barker. *NAM*

49 Death of Sir Thomas Picton. Aquatint by Duborg after J. A. Atkinson. *NAM*

50–51 The field of Waterloo after the battle. Aquatint by M. Duborg after J. Heaviside Clark. *NAM*

54–55 Sir Henry Burrard, attrib. Romney. *NPG*

57 Troops at Torres Vedras. Aquatint by J. Holland. *V & A*

59 Headquarters at Waterloo. Aquatint by Duborg after J. A. Atkinson. *NAM*

60 The retreat to Corruna, by C. R. Beavis. *Parker Gallery*

61 The key of Ciudad Rodrigo. *V & A, Apsley House*

62–63 Marshal Soult, by George Peter Alexander Healy. *V & A*

64 The battle of Oporto by W. Heath. *V & A*

66 Bridge at Miserere. Engraving after H. Leveque. *NAM*

68 The Vitoria battlefield, by T. J. Barker. *Parker Gallery*
69 (*top*) The valley of Vitoria. *Paddy Griffith*
(*centre*) Joseph Bonaparte, by Baron F. P. S. Gérard. *V & A*
(*bottom*) Marshal Jourdan, by Carpentier. *Bulloz, Versailles*
70 Detail from the meeting of Wellington and Blücher, engraving by Lamb Stocks after original wall painting in the Houses of Parliament by D. Maclise. *V & A*
74–75 Baggage of army in India. *NAM*
76 (*above left*) Storming of Seringapatam by W. Heath
(*above right*) Seringapatam gun. *Paddy Griffith, Royal Military Academy, Sandhurst*
(*below*) Storming of Seringapatum. *Parker Gallery*
78–79 Tipoo's sons being handed over as hostages. *Christie's*
81 (*left*) Wellington in Portuguese uniform. Stipple engraving by F. Bartolozzi after D. Pelligrini. *NAM*
(*right*) Beresford. *NAM*
83 Francisco Espoz y Mina. *NAM*
84 Spanish gunner, infantryman and dragoon. *NAM*
86 The Billet, Peninsular War, by R. A. Hillingford. *Courtesy of Mrs Ruth Denton*
87 (*left*) William Prince of Orange. Stipple engraving by W. van Senus after J. Odevare. *NAM*
(*right*) Frederick William III of Prussia by Wilhelm Herbig. *V & A*
90 Intelligence of the Battle of Ligny, by W. Heath. *V & A*
92 Wellington's horse Copenhagen, by B. R. Haydon. *By permission of the Duke of Wellington, Stratfield Saye: photograph Courtauld Institute of Art*
93 (*above*) La Haye Sainte farm. *V & A*
(*below*) La Belle Alliance. *V & A*
95 Map of Austrian Netherlands. *Bibliothèque Royale de Belgique*
96 Blücher under his horse at Waterloo. Lithograph by M. Duborg after J. A. Atkinson. *NAM*
97 La Papelotte farm. *Belgian National Tourist Office, Cliché C.G.T.*
99 Aerial view of battlefield. *Belgian National Tourist Office, Cliché C.G.T.*
100 La Haye Sainte farmyard. *Belgian National Tourist Office, Cliché C.G.T.*
102 La Haye Sainte farmyard. *Belgian National Tourist Office, Cliché C.G.T.*
103 Wellington at Waterloo, by Sullivan. *Parker Gallery*
104 (*facing*) Marshal Ney, by Gérard. *Photo copyright Musée de l'Armée, Paris*
104–5 (*above*) The Battle of Waterloo, by Felix Philippoteaux. *V & A*
(*below*) Napoleon on the evening of the battle of Waterloo, by Ernest Crofts. *Walker Art Gallery*
105 (*facing*) Wellington, by T. Lawrence. *V & A*
106 British square at Quatre Bras. Engraving by R. Josey after Lady Butler. *NAM*
108 Wellington riding through the lines. Watercolour by W. B. Wollen. *NAM*
111 'Take up your bed' – and walk!!!' Satirical cartoon by William Heath. *V & A*
112 Wellington's Waterloo headquarters. *Belgian National Tourist Office, Cliché C.G.T.*
113 Writing the Waterloo despatch. Engraving after original by P. Burghersh. *V & A*
115 Detail from Chatham map. *Royal Engineers Museum, Chatham*
116 The eve of Waterloo, by W. Heath. *Parker Gallery*
117 The morning of the battle, by R. A. Hillingford. *Parker Gallery*
118 Inferno at Hougoumont. From set of four aquatints after A. M. S. engraved by T. Sutherland. *NAM*
119 Wellington's note to Hougoumont garrison. *V & A*
120–1 Repulsing a cavalry charge, by H. Hemy. *Parker Gallery*
123 Last Stand of the Imperial Guard at Waterloo, from painting by R. A. Hillingford. *NAM*
125 Wellington with the Marquess of Anglesey, by C. Colne. *NPG*
126 Napoleon by Robert Lefevre. *V & A*
130 French Encampment, by J. F. Joseph-Swetaèn, called Fontaine. *V & A*
133 Napoleon in 1815, by E. Meissonier. *Musée de l'Armée?*
137 Napoleon at Waterloo. *NAM*
140 The 'Thin Red Line', Balaclava. *NAM*
143 Battle of Talavera by J. Duplessis Bertaux. *V & A*
145 Battle of Assye by W. Heath. *V & A*
146 Battle of Corunna, by W. Heath-Clarke. *Parker Gallery*
147 Battle of the Pyrenees, aquatint by J. C. Stadler after W. Heath. *NAM*
148 Wellington on the field of Waterloo, by J. T. Barker. *Parker Gallery*
151 (*above*) Battle of Busaco. Aquatint by T. Foldry after R. Westall. *NAM*
(*below*) Deployment of a skirmish line. *Courtesy of Hutchinson, London*
152 Horse guards at Battle of Waterloo. Aquatint by Duborg after J. A. Atkinson. *NAM*
153 Busaco. British infantry charging the French. Watercolour by R. Simkin. *NAM*
155 Fuentes de Onoro, by J. Duplessis Bertaux. *V & A*
156 Muskets and locks. *Reproduced by permission of the Board of Trustees of the Armouries, H.M. Tower of London*
158 Two muskets. *Reproduced by permission of the Board of Trustees of the Armouries, H.M. Tower of London*
160 Death of Col. Moorhouse, Madras Artillery, Siege of Bangalore, 1791. Oil by Robert Home. *NAM*
161 Duel of musketry from the Battle of Vimeira aquatint by

Index

(Note that where a place-name is also the title of a battle or siege, the date of the event is cited).